THE BOTTOM LINE

The Bottom Line

**Practical Financial Knowledge
for Managers**

Alan Warner

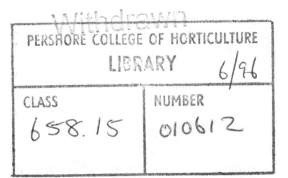
Gower

© Alan Warner 1988

First published 1988 by Gower Publishing Company Limited,
Aldershot, Hampshire

This paperback edition published 1993
Gower Publishing
Gower House
Croft Road
Aldershot
Hants GU11 3HR
England

Gower
Old Post Road
Brookfield
Vermont 05036
U.S.A.

Reprinted 1995

CIP catalogue records for this book are available from the
British Library

ISBN 0 566 07480 X

Printed in Great Britain at the University Press, Cambridge

Summary of Content

Chapter 1

I gaze out of my office window at the loading bay below. Giant lorries queue up to get in and the air is riddled with shouts of frustration and impatience. The driver of Kwikmart Supermarket's enormous lorry is arguing with one of our drivers who wants to load his vehicle first to take an inter-company delivery. The Despatch Manager tries to arbitrate but they both claim loading priority.

I think nostalgically back to the days when business was fun. Being down at the loading bay early in the morning to laugh and chat with the bread roundsmen before they set off was a favourite pastime. The air would be full of jokes and innuendos about the women who were waiting on the rounds, no arguments about who got to the loading bay first. But that was when our products – bread, cakes and pies – were sold at the home and the corner shop, not in impersonal supermarkets. That was before the governor sold out to Universal. That was before the accountants took over.

The Kwikmart man wins, as usual – these multiples are powerful enough to win every battle these days – and prepares to take his giant load, bound for their central distribution point. I turn to my desk and look unhappily at the mountain of paper which now seems to represent my main work task. Being Sales and Marketing Director used to mean meeting people, mixing with the lads, entertaining customers, chairing meetings which really got things done. Now it seems to mean taking part in a paperchase with the main objective of keeping Head Office happy. Filling in forms for budgets, cashflows, latest estimates and responding to incessant requests for explanations and more data.

Still, mustn't become self-pitying, I am after all a success. Sales and Marketing Director of the town's biggest firm and with an outside chance of being the next Managing Director, though Universal are expected to put their man in – they usually do a few years after acquisition. Yes, I am a success, but then I've worked for it – and it ruined my marriage.

As if on cue, Maggie, my latest secretary and latest *affaire*, comes to remind me of today's appointments. John Appleby, Production Director, to discuss next quarter's production forecasts at 9.30, annual appraisal meeting with the MD at 11.30, and lunch with the new Management Accountant from Universal, who starts today. I ask Maggie what a management accountant is but her expression shows that she does not regard answering such questions as part of her job description.

"Where am I meeting Appleby?" I ask, and find that it's in his office in the factory. I decide to leave straight away even though it's only 9.00 because, that way, I can avoid the paper pile for another day.

"Got that Monday morning feeling?" asks Maggie as I leave. "You weren't so quiet yesterday morning." I remind myself that I should avoid relationships with my secretaries. I used to be very critical of those who mixed their work and their love lives in the days when I was a family man, the envy of the firm with a lovely wife and two kids.

As I walk past the despatch department I see the Kwikmart driver directing our loaders, "Who's running this business?" I ask myself.

Appleby always tries to arrange meetings in his office – it seems to help his campaign to make me feel inferior to him, which he usually succeeds in doing despite my greater age, status and seniority. I used to take part in subtle battles and always assume he would come to me but recently I've decided it's not worth it. It does me good to see the factory anyway – it's easy to forget the problems of the men on the shop floor. There are still a lot of faces I know and

I wave as I go past. But it's not like the old days when I would stop for a chat. The automated processes and Appleby's insistence on productivity at the expense of all else have taken away any chance of socializing.

Appleby really is too clever by half. A bumptious young engineer, put in by Universal, obviously very bright and ambitious but totally devoid of humour and humanity. He's been with us for two years, during which time all the efficiency ratios have increased and all the unit costs have gone down. His staff think he's a bastard but have a sneaking admiration for him. I tend to share their view but the admiration is strictly limited. Still, we need to get on together so I try to hide my views, but I keep the relationship on a strictly businesslike footing.

He has rimless spectacles and a small head with a slightly receding hairline, exuding as much warmth and humanity as the computer on his desk. He is working on his computer as I walk in and he appears not to notice me for a few seconds. I suspect that really he knows I'm there and this is all part of his image.

"Oh, hello, Phil," he says. "Come and sit down. I'm just finalizing the optimum product mix calculation for next quarter."

I spend the next hour listening to Applebly, or at least pretending to listen, while he explains his calculations. He shows me his computer, using his spreadsheet as he calls it, explaining why we must push much harder on pie sales next quarter. Once he calls in the Cost Accountant, Mike Marshall, who seems to spend all his time in Appleby's department even though technically he is supposed to give me cost information too. Not that I really need or want it – I believe in keeping things simple and my sales figures are all that really interest me.

At about 10.30 the meeting comes to a halt. I agree with Appleby about next quarter's forecasts and promise to encourage pie sales as much as possible by applying quotas and sales incentive schemes. Otherwise I know that the sales force will ignore what we say and go for bread sales because that's where sales are easiest to achieve and the commission most quickly earned.

Just as I get out of the door he says, "I've got this new management accountant coming to see me at 11 o'clock. Are you seeing him?" I reply that I'm seeing him for lunch. "What's it all about, do you know?" asks Appleby. "I'm quite happy with Mike without anyone else being sent in from Universal."

I tell him that I have no feelings either way and maybe it's just Head Office's way of ensuring that we follow all their reporting systems.

"Yes," he says, "you may be right. I heard that Universal weren't happy with old Berisford's profit and cash forecasts." Berisford is the Chief Accountant, who's been with us for forty years and is nearing retirement. He is basically a book-keeper and has not adapted easily to the acquisition.

I don't feel like going back to the office to face Maggie's hints or the pile of paper so I decide to visit the sales office until it's time to see Jim Lawrence, the MD, at 11.30. There was a time when this was part of my morning routine. What has changed? Why did it seem a good use of my time then but rarely now? Perhaps Universal and the young Turks like Appleby have made me believe that only figures and paper are worth spending time on.

After spending the hour chatting to a number of staff in the sales office, I feel convinced that I should go out of my office more often. I find out more in that hour than in a whole week's paper shuffling. I learn that the trends of pie orders are moving steadily down and Harper, the young Order Processing Manager, is concerned about our plans to buck the trend. He fears that the salesmen's time will be distracted from the mainstream bread and cake lines. He also tells me that the amount of administrative and manage-ment time taken up with looking into queries and other hassles with Kwikmart is affecting our ability to deal with other customers. He says that, from what he hears about the discounts they are getting, we probably make no money at all from them, despite the high volume.

I make for Jim Lawrence's office for my annual appraisal without much hope that it will achieve very much. Jim only does appraisals because it's now required by Universal – he seems to find it all a bit embarrassing and usually gets it over as quickly as possible. This time I won't let him get away with it. I'll tell him what I think about how things are going and pin him down about my future, in particular my chances of getting his job. I'm not sure I'll like the answer – but what have I got to lose?

Chapter 2

Jim's secretary, Sylvia, looks at me disapprovingly. "Mr Lawrence is on the phone to Head Office, Mr Moorley," she says.

It's always Mr Moorley these days – we used to be on Christian name terms but she's been very distant since my divorce. I ask myself whether it's because she's just about the only secretary I haven't made a pass at during these last three years of freedom, and then hate myself for thinking it. Sylvia is just one of those people who values loyalty, the sort that she's shown to Jim these thirty years she's worked for him. The break up of my marriage disillusioned her as it disillusioned many others – how could it happen to that perfectly happy couple?

I don't mind waiting for Jim. I know what it's like when Head Office are on the phone. Prior, the Universal Director responsible for our company, regards all other meetings and appointments as secondary to his needs and expects immediate response. I've even seen Jim called out of meetings to answer his never-ending stream of queries.

As I enter Jim's office ten minutes later, the pressure on him is all too evident on his face. I wonder if this is what he anticipated when he left school and joined the family business, named "Lawrensons" by his father to anticipate his son's eventual partnership. Jim's father, Gustav, came to England from Poland during the second World War and, from the beginnings of a stall in the local market, built a successful business on the principles of quality food products. Gustav sold out to Universal five years ago, shortly before he died, to protect Jim and the rest of the family from tax problems and to provide security for their future after his death. This was a terrible blow to Jim but he recognized the inevitability of it and was glad he didn't have to be the one to make the decision.

"Come in, Phil," he says. "Sorry to keep you waiting – how are things?"

I know that he doesn't want a reply, that's his standard greeting. Jim and I know each other as well as any two people who work together can know each other, after twenty-five years as close colleagues. Yet, in other ways, we don't know each other at all, no social contact, no real communication except what is necessary to do the job in hand. What we do share, however, is a belief that together we made Lawrensons what it is, after the old man got it off the ground in the nineteen-fifties.

"Now what's this meeting about?" he says, showing his embarrassment. "Oh yes, this appraisal thing. I suppose we must do it. Seems silly for us, doesn't it, but we must set an example. Come and sit over here."

We sit in the easy chairs at the far end of his enormous office. I feel a certain envy, comparing it to my rather poky one, and wonder if I still have a chance to make it mine.

We chat vaguely for a while, going over how things have been progressing. Sylvia has produced the file with the objectives we agreed and we talk our way through the problems which have arisen during the year. I know that my performance hasn't been as good as it could have been, but if Jim is aware of it he doesn't show it. He is a shy person deep down, and finds overt criticism as difficult as he finds giving praise, so we talk around the main issue. I know that the real problem is that I've lost the drive and enthusiasm which I brought to Lawrensons when I left school in 1960 and which I gave them for over twenty years.

"Well, Phil, thanks for coming," Jim says. "I must get on unless you've got anything else. Draft out some objectives for next year and we'll meet again to approve them."

He begins to get up but I stay put.

"No Jim," I say, "I've got some important issues I want to discuss. Two, in fact. And the appraisal is supposed to be the time when we discuss the really important things, isn't it?"

He looks at his watch.

"All right, Phil, but I have a lunch appointment so don't beat around the bush."

I take a deep breath.

"Well, Jim, firstly I want to talk about the way things are going here. The place just isn't like it used to be. People are becoming cowed and there's no enjoyment any more. The Applebys of this world are taking over – it's all return on capital, operating cash flow and all that crap, without any thought about what the firm means to the people like us who made it what it is. And Universal's pressure for profit makes us cut back on all the long-term things like product development and training which can always wait till next year. We'd never have allowed that to happen in the old days, Jim."

He looks embarrassed and scratches his bald pate. "You said there were two issues?" he says, his tone betraying slight impatience.

"Yes, the second is my future. I'm only forty-three, Jim, and you're retiring in three years. We've never talked about my chances of succession and I think it's time we did. Because I'm not sure I want to work in this job for another seventeen years to collect my pension."

He gets up and looks out of the window.

"Do you want to hear it straight, Phil?" he asks and I nod.

"We've been friends for a long time, Phil, and it's about time you heard a few home truths. I suppose I'm the only one who can do it. Of course things are different. The old man sold out – it had to happen some time and we now have to live in the real world. Do you think I enjoy being besieged by Prior and his army of accountants for monthly profit and cash flow forecasts? But they own the bloody place now, Phil, and nostalgia for yesterday's fun and games isn't going to change anything. All right, sometimes we do have to sacrifice the long term to make this year's profits and believe me I do try to fight that battle with Head Office. But they have their shareholders who are not always as patient as we'd like them to be. The best thing we can do is to make even more profit so we can afford to spend for the future and still make the returns that Universal want. And that means putting a lot more energy into your job than you showed last year."

I swallow hard. "But you said my performance had been OK."

"Yes," he says, "but that was me backing off as usual to avoid hurting your feelings. You wanted it straight and you're getting it. You've bloody well irritated me."

It's over ten years since anyone has spoken to me like this and then it was Jim's father. I open my mouth but there's no stopping him now. "And as for my job, three years ago I would have said you were favourite for it, but you have no chance unless you pull yourself together. In any case it won't be my decision."

"No," I say, "but your recommendation will surely be crucial."

"Maybe, but at the moment I wouldn't recommend you. You're behaving like yesterday's man. And there are two other problems."

I'm beginning to wish I hadn't started this.

"I'm sorry to say this, Phil, but there is your personal life. I know it's only relevant if it affects your position here but it's beginning to do just that. I don't usually listen to gossip, but, ever since you and Jean split up, there have been lots of stories about you. Whether they're true or not, you could not have an MD here who is, not to put too fine a point on it, playing around with the secretaries. Whatever happened to you and Jean?"

I would like to tell him that she left because I gave those years when the children were growing up to him and his father, helping them to make their fortune and sell out. But he isn't in the mood for listening now and he wouldn't understand anyway. His family could never see any conflict between home and job – his wife would always be waiting for him if he worked sixteen hours a day, which he frequently did.

"And there's another reason, which you could do something about. As you said, the accountants dominate at Universal and, like it or not, that's the reality. They need men at the top who think in those terms. I'm really struggling but they'll put up with me for my last three years. But the next MD will have to be able to understand these financial terms like the bottom line that Prior's always going on about."

"Do you mean that the next MD will be an accountant? God help us all."

"No," Jim replies, "but he will be someone who at least knows what they are talking about and gives as good as he gets."

"Like Appleby, I suppose?"

"Well, not Appleby. He's too young and has no vision. But someone of his type, put in by Universal. It's my bet at the moment that they'll put in someone from another company or from Head Office. Unless you do something about what I've told you."

"But I'm no accountant, Jim, you know that."

"I know you're not. But you could at least get yourself trained to understand these financial things. I'm too long in the tooth but you have time. And you're pretty bright at numbers – I remember when we used to sell pies together, you would always add up the bill."

I smile at the memory and realize that I deserve all this. I had it coming to me. When I get up to leave his office a few minutes later, I feel strange, as if an enormous load has been lifted from me. I now see myself as others see me and, though I don't like what I see, I feel refreshed. I now have something to aim for. I'll show the Applebys of this world a thing or two.

"Thanks, Jim," I say, "what you've said has been very helpful. I'll work on things."

"Good. Perhaps these appraisals aren't such a bad thing, after all."

As I walk out of the door he asks, "By the way, have you met our new Management Accountant?"

"No," I say, "I'm just meeting him for lunch now. Is he a Head Office plant?"

He looks amused and surprised.

"I think I'll leave you to make your own judgement,"

he says, "but remember that an accountant may help you with at least one of your problems. And I think you might be in for a surprise with this one."

Chapter 3

I walk back to my office thinking about accountants. When I first joined Lawrensons we had an old chap called Stubbins as Chief Accountant and he was no trouble. He was very much in the same mould as Berisford, produced the accounts at the end of the year, paid our expenses and occasionally chased us for an invoice. We used to laugh about him because he was your typical boring accountant and when Jean saw the *Monty Python* send up, she said – "that's old Stubbins!" – the sort of chap who would be really excited about a row of beans to count.

I think of all the other adjectives I've associated with accountants I've known over the years – cautious, negative, secretive, in many cases arrogant, particularly the young chartered accountants who appear for the audit each year. All public school types with that irritating confidence which comes from being in 'the profession' as they call it.

Since the takeover by Universal, I've seen accountants in a different, more sinister, light. The adjectives are more like dominating, rigid, tight-fisted – I feel glad that I didn't listen to my Dad and become one. Give me sales and marketing any day – at least we're positive, achieving things, earning money, not just holding everyone back.

I shall forget about accountants. Jim has given a new meaning to my career at Lawrensons and I'm going to make him sit up – obviously he's written me off. Oh no, I can't forget about accountants because I'm lunching with one – Chris

Goodhart, the new Management Accountant from Universal. I wish I wasn't but there was no other way I could fit him in this week – I wonder where Maggie's fixed lunch?

"In the dining room, in the private area," she tells me when I get back. I wonder how I'm going to pass an hour or so talking to a bean counter.

I'm hanging around in Maggie's office, looking at the morning messages, when the door opens and in walks this girl. I suppose it's my advancing middle age which makes me call all females younger than me girls, because really she's a woman in every sense of the word. Mid-twenties I suppose, fairly tall, long blond hair, attractive in a baby-doll sort of way. For a moment she reminds me of Lady Penelope, one of the Thunderbird puppets I used to love watching with the kids. She's one of those women who's attractive in every sense but without sex appeal. Perhaps her business-like air, her grey suit and the briefcase she's carrying create this impression.

Maggie and I both look at her wondering why she's here. Maggie asks, "Can I help you?"

"Yes, I've come to see Mr Moorley. Is this his office?"

"This is Mr Moorley," says Maggie and I nod to her, "but I'm afraid you'll need an appointment."

"I have one," she says. "I've started here as Management Accountant today. Didn't my secretary fix a lunch meeting?"

I decide to do a bit of covering up. "Come into my office," I say. "We were expecting you but we just overlooked it for a moment." I wonder if I sound as embarrassed as I feel?

I take her in and she sits opposite my desk. She smiles a confident smile which says "Don't try looking down at me, I'm an equal."

"Well, you're not quite what I expected," I say and know immediately that it sounds patronizing. But she doesn't seem to mind and that smile comes back again, with a direct look into my eyes that makes mine shift away. I decide to come clean.

"Actually I thought you were a fellow, I just heard the name Chris Goodhart and never thought anything else. Christine, I assume?"

"Yes, but I prefer Chris and you're not the first to make the mistake."

I guess that she's enjoying my embarrassment and probably does nothing to prevent such misunderstandings happening. Our new Management Accountant could be a force to be reckoned with.

Fifteen minutes later, as we leave for lunch I'm still thinking the same. She's a confident lady who doesn't allow herself to be dominated in conversation and who asks as many questions as she answers. I'm beginning to enjoy talking to her. Can this really be a bean counter?

As we enter the dining room, heads turn and people look back to their lunch partners and start whispering. I can guess what they're saying. "Who is she? The new accountant? You watch him, anything in a skirt, you know; did you know his wife? Lovely girl, he didn't deserve her." They're probably right but I hate them for saying it.

After we've ordered, I try to find out how someone like this has ended up as an accountant.

"I read history at Durham University." I raise my eyebrows in surprise. "I suppose you think I should have a maths degree but, in fact, I struggled to get 'O' level maths. People don't realize that you don't necessarily have to be good at maths to be an accountant. And vice versa. Some highly numerate people make very bad accountants."

"Tell me more about that. I'm not sure I know what an accountant really does."

"OK, but let me tell you more about the way I came into it. It might help you understand what I mean."

She tells me how in her last year at university she decided that she wanted to make a career in business because degrees in history don't leave many options open and she felt it was right for her personality. She wanted badly to be successful in something and business seemed to provide the best opportunities for women.

On the "milk round" of large organizations looking for graduate management trainees she chose Universal because it provided a broad business training and had a reputation for the excellence of its management. She went into one of their subsidiaries in the ice cream business and spent a few months in each of the functions – personnel, sales, marketing, production, distribution and accounting. Then, after eighteen months, each trainee had to specialise for the early part of their career.

"What made you choose accounting?" I ask. "I would have thought personnel or marketing would have suited you better."

"More suitable for a woman?" she chides, but goes on to explain. "I felt that accounting had more potential, particularly management accounting. Because very few people seemed to be doing it well or to be thinking about why they were doing it and I seemed to have some flair for it. Though I was no good at school maths, I'm quick with figures and can see numerical relationships easily, which is far more important. Also I think I'm quite a good communicator and that's about ninety per cent of the job of a management accountant anyway."

I'm even more sure now that I don't know what an accountant does, so I ask her to explain what all the terms mean: auditor, accountant, management accountant.

"Well," she says, "it's rather complicated, but I'll do my best. There are chartered accountants, whose prime role is to audit a company's accounts and check that the figures produced by the company are what they call 'true and fair'. Their function is to protect the shareholders by ensuring that management don't manipulate the figures for their own ends, like failing to make provisions for bad debts and overstating profits, that sort of thing. I'm not a chartered accountant because you have to have several years of being articled and I could never have put up with the boredom of ticking ledgers. Essentially it's a negative, checking role, rather than a forward-looking one, like the management accountant."

"But surely chartered accountants do work in industry, don't they?"

"Yes, they do and they're very much in demand. I often wonder why, because their training doesn't always make them right for industry's needs. But they are often very high calibre people and, once they've qualified, they have to decide whether to stay in a professional practice and spend a career in auditing, which is quite lucrative, or to move into industry and take a job, either in financial or management accounting."

"Now you're confusing me again," I say. "What's the difference between financial and management accounting?"

"Well, the financial accountant is the one who keeps the books which the auditors later check. Not the basic routine, because that's done by book-keepers and nowadays by computer, but the management of the people who carry out the work and the accounting judgements which are negotiated with the auditors. They are also often responsible for managing the cash, though this treasury function is now often done by specialists, particularly in big companies."

I understand why she said it was complicated but I'm enjoying talking to her and it keeps the conversation going. I concentrate on looking at her mouth because I find her eyes so clear and challenging that I can't look at them. I like the way she seems to be able to talk and smile at the same time.

"But are these financial accountants all chartered?" I ask.

"No, some are not qualified at all. You shouldn't think that being qualified is everything. All it really proves is that you're good at passing exams and probably bloody awful at communicating. Anyone who can lock themselves away for four years and cram all that information into their mind is unlikely to be very socially inclined."

"I can't see you in the financial accounting role," I say.

"No, again it's essentially historical, needing care and conservatism, which are not really my scene. It's a most important function but I find management accounting more rewarding."

"What sort of qualification do you need to be a management accountant then?"

"Again I don't think qualifications are that vital – an understanding of business and good communication skills are much more important. Some chartered accountants move across to it but the main body is The Institute of Cost and Management Accountants, which I belong to. I don't really think the exams did me much good, but Universal like their management accountants to have letters after their name and it increases my job prospects. But some of the best management accountants I've seen around are not qualified as accountants at all, probably economics graduates or MBAs."

I ought to ask her what an MBA is but I'm embarrassed that I don't know and don't want to stop her when she's in full flow.

"In other European countries where they're not so obsessed with qualifications, there are successful management accountants who see business in a very broad sense. Some of Universal's people in France and Germany are quite brilliant. You wouldn't recognize them as accountants at all because you're so influenced by the *Monty Python* stereotype and the image of the boring chartered accountant."

I'm surprised she's heard of *Monty Python* – is she old enough to remember? – and encourage her to tell me more. I'm actually becoming interested – Moorley interested in a description of the accounting profession? Absurd, but I keep on listening.

"Just what does the management accountant do?" I ask her.

"Well, she's different," she says with a smile. "She isn't required to protect the shareholders or to keep the books. I'm only worth employing if I present financial information which helps management to make good decisions. Management accounting involves giving people like you the means to see the financial implications of what you're doing. That's why communication skills are so important. I've got to sell the idea to you and your colleagues. To prove that you can get better information and educate you how to use it."

"I've never thought of accountants as salesmen or educators."

"Well, things are going to change, Mr Moorley, because the sales and marketing function is the one where I think I can be of most use. I'm not sure about production. Mr Appleby seems to think he has all the data he needs and that I can't help him. I was hoping that you might be more amenable."

"Please call me Phil," I say, "I'm willing to give it a try. I'm determined to make changes in our operations – we've been standing still in sales and marketing for too long and it's my fault. Maybe you'll be able to help me."

"If I can't, all my training will have been wasted. I think we could work well together."

Chapter 4

The next day I'm sitting at my desk, having a working lunch brought in by Maggie. I've decided to miss the usual visit to the Red Lion and start to work through my bulging in-tray. Only when I'm up to date can I start things moving in the way I want and thus prove Jim Lawrence wrong.

I think about Chris for about the tenth time this morning – never will bean counters be the same again for me. It's not just that she's attractive – though she's not really my type, I tell myself – but she genuinely seems to want to help, something I've never associated with accountants. But, as she told me, Lawrensons have never really had a management accountant before.

Before we finished lunch, she told me that her ultimate ambition was to go to the States to get an MBA at an American Business School. Apparently MBA stands for Master of Business Administration and is a postgraduate degree for those who wish to broaden their experience and prepare for a career in general management. I learned that, though many UK and other European institutions now award MBAs, there is much more choice in the States. The American MBA will have much more career clout, particularly if she can achieve her dream of going to Harvard.

Later on we were talking about my problems with Appleby and how he seems to dominate my marketing plans with his complicated product mix analyses. Chris seemed interested in this and I gave her the next quarter's forecast before she left.

Just as I'm drafting out my plans for the salesmen's quotas and product allocations, the phone rings. It's Chris.

"Hi," she says, "sorry to bother you at lunch. In fact I didn't really expect to get you."

"No problem, but don't management accountants have lunch breaks either?"

"Phil," she says, ignoring my question and going straight to the point, "I need to see you urgently about the information you gave me yesterday. Before you do anything to implement that product mix plan."

"Why, has Appleby got it wrong?"

"Possibly, but I need further data. When are you free?"

"About 4.30."

"Fine, and could you dig out last quarter's results for the three main product groups for us to look at? OK? Thanks. Bye."

I put the phone down and wonder what she's up to. Appleby's no fool and taking him on could be a dodgy business. Even though Chris is bright, she's fairly inexperienced and doesn't know much about our business yet. Anyway, I look for the paper she wants, prepared recently by Mike Marshall the Cost Accountant. It looks like this.

Profit and loss account (£'000)

£'000	Bread	Pies	Cakes	Total
Sales	11,450	7,880	7,430	26,760
Direct costs				
Materials	3,670	4,110	2,300	10,080
Direct labour	1,820	840	1,200	3,860
Energy	360	270	340	970
Repairs	120	280	140	540
Distribution	640	500	470	1,610
Consumables	90	70	70	230
Indirect labour	190	160	170	520
Depreciation	360	340	310	1,010
Management	140	120	120	380
Others	60	40	40	140
Total direct costs	7,450	6,730	5,160	19,340
Profit before indirects	4,000	1,150	2,270	7,420
Allocation of indirects	2,840	2,040	2,060	6,940
Profit/(loss)	1,160	(890)	210	480

I haven't actually studied it before. Like all the financial data which Berisford and Marshall produce, it just goes into my out-tray. I wonder why? Is it just because I can't handle figures as Jim Lawrence suggested, and therefore avoid them at all costs? Or is it because I've never tried? Or maybe it's the way they're presented – I have no problem with the sales statistics which the sales admin. department produces, particularly the graphs of sales volumes, but they are done to suit my needs.

Just before Chris comes at 4.30, I have another look at the figures. How can Appleby be wrong? We are losing money on pies because of the problems of achieving volume. It's become such a competitive market recently with so many supermarkets moving into their own in-store bakeries. But we can increase volume by sales and marketing effort and we must do something to get over breakeven.

She comes in, dead on time, her face even more doll-like than yesterday, her blue eyes clear and direct, her blond hair immaculately groomed, swinging and shining like the shampoo adverts.

She looks businesslike and enthusiastic. How can she be so excited about columns of figures? Perhaps it's just the keenness which people show when they're in a new job until the cynics like me wear them down. I bring her to my table and we sit down. I give her a copy of the profit and loss account.

She looks at it and we discuss some detailed points. She asks me about my selling and marketing costs, which are included in the allocation of indirects. She asks me how they are split between different product groups and the effect on these costs of increased volume. She asks how I manage to influence product mix by fixing salesmen's quotas, giving them incentives or using sales instructions.

She also wants to know about some of Appleby's costs but I can't really help her. I tell her she will have to see Appleby or Marshall. From the look on her face I see that she won't find that easy. She is obviously having trouble with those two and I'm not surprised. I'm growing concerned for her and I try to warn her of the dangers of challenging people too quickly.

"Chris," I say, "are you sure you ought to be doing this so soon? Whatever I think of Appleby, he does seem to know what he's doing and Jim Lawrence said at last month's management meeting that we had to bring pies up to breakeven. I can't see how you can argue with that."

"I need to do some more work, Phil, but I think I can. It's rather complicated to explain at this stage but it's to do with the way costs behave and achieving the best financial return from your salesmen's efforts. Isn't that what you want?"

"Yes, of course, but if we get pies into breakeven, we shall transform our profits." I point out on the sheet that bread and cakes together make £1,370 profit per quarter without the loss from pies.

"Phil," she asks, "what do you know about cost behaviour?" Again she ignores what I say and asks her own question. With most others in Lawrensons I wouldn't put up with it but somehow with this lady it doesn't seem to matter.

"Not a lot, but I'm sure you're about to tell me."

"OK, but first of all – why does this profit and loss account show direct costs, with profit before indirects and then indirects?"

"I don't know. I think it came in when Universal took us over. Up until then we didn't have much costing. Stubbins and Berisford just added up all the expenses each quarter, took them off sales and calculated profit. Isn't this way, direct and indirect, the Universal system?"

"Yes," she replies, "but that's for reporting to Universal House. They have to have standard formats for their central systems but they're in so many industries – soaps, animal feeds, chemicals – that they can't possibly dictate a standard format for your costing. That should be geared to what you need to help your decisions."

"Does it matter? The information seems OK to me."

"I'm not so sure. Tell me, what is a direct cost as far as you're concerned?" I hesitate, embarrassed that I've never really thought about it and anxious not to make myself look foolish. "One that's... sort of... directly... related to the product, I suppose."

"Right. Related to, identifiable with, attributable to. That's the idea. But why do you think these costs are separated from the other costs, the indirects?"

I really ought to be irritated by someone, new to the company, questioning me like this but I'm not. She's so earnest and enthusiastic that I can't object. And I think back to my meeting with Jim. Maybe this is the way to improve my financial knowledge, asking Chris to explain the jargon and break down some of the mystique. There's no point in pretending to know it all.

"Look, Chris," I say, "I don't really know much about these things. I just follow the system. I've never thought about why they're split between direct and indirect. As I said, it's the Universal system. You should know why they do it."

"OK," she says, "I'll tell you, though I honestly think some of the people at Universal don't know themselves. It's just an end in itself to many of them. But the real reason should be longer-term guidance, to assess how the management are performing, to compare Universal companies in similar industries and decide where to invest and where to pull out. OK?"

I nod my head in agreement and she continues. "Yet here you are using the same structure to work out the best product mix for next quarter, a very different short-term tactical decision. And you're placing a lot of reliance on the direct/indirect split when many of the apportionments of indirect costs are likely to be quite arbitrary."

"We don't really place that much reliance on the apportionments. We all know they're dependent on many assumptions."

"But you do, Phil, don't you see? The loss on pies is only what it is because of these apportionments!"

Looking at the figures I can see that she has a point. Evidently I'm going to learn a lot from our new Management Accountant. She carries on talking, sensing that I'm on her side now.

"Phil, have you heard of fixed and variable costs? Do you know the difference between the two?"

I vaguely remember hearing about this on a finance for

non-financial managers course about ten years ago, but it's a dim and distant memory. I won't pretend that I really know, as I often do at management meetings, because Chris does seem to want to help. She told me over lunch yesterday how an accountant should educate colleagues to understand financial information. I like the idea, particularly when the teacher is as attractive as this one.

"Not properly, Chris," I reply. "I've heard people refer to fixed costs at meetings. Is it those which can be controlled within budget?"

"No, that's controllable cost which is another useful approach in some circumstances. The fixed and variable split concerns the relationship to sales volume."

Chris is in full cry now, the mission to explain shining out of her eyes as she walks to the flipchart in the corner of my office. She looks wonderful from the back, with her blond hair, her slim body and her shapely legs. With an effort I return to what she's saying.

"Fixed costs are those which stay the same in money terms, whatever the volume in the short term. We're both fixed costs – our salaries are the same whatever the amount we sell or produce."

"I'm not so sure about that, Chris. Universal would soon discard us if volume went down enough. And if volume, say, doubled, we'd be unable to cope and we'd need more people."

"OK. I'm not saying that it's a definition which is valid over the very long term or for big changes in volume. It's just a convenient definition for looking at the short term, like this decision you're making about next quarter's product mix. What would you call a fixed cost in those circumstances?"

"Rent, rates, admin., all our selling expenses I suppose, research and development."

"But you told me that the salesmen are on commission?"

"Yes, of course, that wouldn't be fixed, would it? And I'm not sure about advertising because, as I told you, we allocate the yearly spend based on volume."

"Yes, I need to look at that in more detail, but you've got the general idea about fixed costs. Variable costs are obviously those that aren't fixed – those where the amount spent does move with volume. You can only define these accurately after examining in detail how costs behave in each business. Which other costs do you think are variable in addition to commission, taking all costs, not just your own? Which ones vary more or less with sales volume?"

"Well, clearly materials, most of the energy costs in Appleby's area, I suppose. Some of the distribution costs, because we subcontracted part of the operation to a specialist company last year. And probably some more of Appleby's overheads."

"What about wage costs? You've left those out."

"Yes, I wasn't sure. My sales force is certainly fixed, apart from the commission. And so are the admin. and secretaries. As I said earlier, I don't know much about the factory operation but I should think it's mainly variable. There's a lot of casual work and overtime which we've always used to balance labour cost and demand. Though I did hear that Appleby was thinking of taking on more permanent staff and buying more equipment to cut out the overtime and casuals. Look, Chris, why is all this so important?"

"Well," she says, standing by the flipchart, marker pen in hand, "for short-term operating decisions like how to make maximum profit this quarter, you must know which costs are going to move with volume and which are not. Otherwise you will be making judgements about volume levels and product mix without evaluating the financial consequences. And I think that's exactly what you're doing here. I need to go back to Appleby and do some more analysis, but I hope to surprise both of you."

"All right, I'll look forward to that but please be careful. Appleby doesn't take kindly to being challenged. And I'm not even sure I'm convinced. I still don't see how any split between fixed and variable costs can be any good unless it's accurate, and surely it all depends on the time period you assume. Aren't all costs variable in the long term?"

"Yes, of course you're right – nothing is ever perfect. The distinction between fixed and variable is always subject to challenge but, as I hope to show you, even an approximate split can be helpful. And bear in mind that we're talking about short-term decisions. That's the context where this approach is the most powerful."

She starts to draw on the flipchart. I sit back rather like a little boy with his favourite teacher. I notice that it's past six o'clock and remember that I've promised to take Maggie out, but I decide that I'll let Chris carry on. There's something compelling about her interest and commitment which makes me reluctant to stop her. She's drawn a graph. Who ever heard of an accountant doing that?

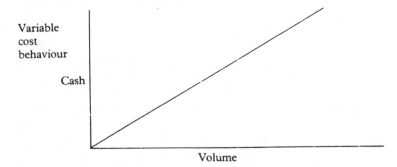

"OK," she says – I notice that OK is a favourite phrase of hers – "that's the behaviour of the variable cost. It may not be entirely linear because you may be able, say, to buy better at higher volume, but it's near enough. The fixed cost looks like this."

I expect to see a straight line with volume but she draws something different.

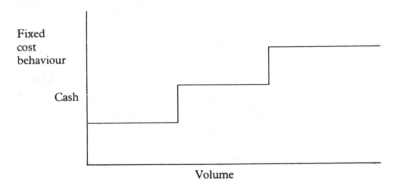

"You see, Phil," she explains, "a fixed cost is really one which varies in steps rather than in a direct line. But we use the distinction to make decisions within the timeframe of each step. Once you go beyond, I agree that fixed/variable costing may not be the best approach."

She looks at her watch. "I must be going," she says. "I'm going to the theatre tonight."

I wonder who she's going with? I won't ask. Surely this girl must be spoken for, though I've already observed that there's no ring on her third finger. I remember what Jim told me about my reputation as a womanizer and decide that this is one relationship which I'll keep on a strictly business basis.

We agree to meet in two days' time and she gets up to leave.

"Chris," I say, "before you go, can you tell me one thing? What does the bottom line mean? All the Universal people go on about it and I'm never quite sure which level of profit they're referring to."

"It's just a cliché," she says, "just another phrase for profit, though it can be used in other contexts. I suppose that its final definition is profit after tax, what's left for the share-holders."

"I thought that was earnings."

"Yes, it is. Earnings is just another word for profit, too, though in the Stock Exchange it normally means profit after tax. If you like, we can have a session together and I'll define all the jargon for you."

"I'd like that," I say. "It's the jargon which causes half of the problems for me."

After she's gone, I go into the outer office and there, on Maggie's typewriter, for all to see, is a note:

I THOUGHT WE WERE GOING FOR A DRINK AT SIX. YOU OBVIOUSLY PREFER YOUR NEW ACCOUNTANT'S COMPANY TO MINE. YOU CAN COOK YOUR OWN SUPPER AND SLEEP IN YOUR OWN BED

MAGGIE

Anyone who came into the office could have seen the note and certainly the office cleaners would have enjoyed reading it. I wonder if Chris saw it when she went out? I'm going to have to do something about Maggie and quickly.

Chapter 5

Exactly a week later, I'm in my office again working late, looking out of my window at the big vans loading for their night deliveries. Realizing yet again that I spend too much time in the office, I've decided to set aside some days in my diary when I can go out into the field and get to know what our customers are thinking. I buzz for my new secretary, Miss Brooks, who has been brought out of retirement to help me after Maggie's sudden departure. Miss Brooks seems glad to be needed again and will work any hours I need her.

It was hard on Maggie but she took it well. The settlement was far more than she'd get at a tribunal and Jim was happy to approve it on condition that I was genuinely cleaning up my act. Since she's gone I've had a feeling of release and a determination to keep my work and personal life well apart. The nights are lonely but I reckon, if I throw myself into my job, I can live with that. I saw the kids at the weekend and took them to a film, though, as usual, Jean and I hardly spoke when I picked them up and dropped them off. Her bitterness seems deeper than ever.

Miss Brooks comes in, bristling with efficiency, diary and notebook in hand. I ask her to fix the date with the sales force and she puts some papers on my desk.

"This top one is from Miss Goodhart. She says it's the printout she promised to circulate after yesterday's management meeting."

I pick it up.

Quarterly profit and loss account ('000)

	Bread	Pies	Cakes	Total
Sales	11,450	7,880	7,430	26,760
Variable costs				
Materials	3,670	4,110	2,300	10,080
Labour	1,820	840	1,200	3,860
Energy	360	270	340	970
Repairs	120	280	140	540
Distribution	640	500	470	1,610
Consumables	90	70	70	230
Commission	246	186	204	636
Total	6,946	6,256	4,724	17,926
Contribution	4,504	1,624	2,706	8,834
Contrib. %	39.3%	20.6%	36.4%	33.0%
Fixed production costs				2,050
Profit before fixed indirects				6,784
Fixed indirects				6,304
Profit/loss				480

I think back over the last seven days and how Chris has made her mark. First she beat Appleby at his own game, using the computer to show him that his plan to sell more pies next quarter was not the way to give us maximum profitability. She had already shown me, before we went to Appleby, that selling more bread and cake, in that order, would make more money for the company as a whole.

"Phil," she said, "if you had a shop with three products on the counter, one making 40 per cent and one making 20 per cent, you wouldn't have much doubt which to sell given the choice, would you? That's exactly what these contribution percentages tell you. You take off the variable costs from the sales to get contribution, and the percentage represents the extra profit from £100 extra sales of each product."

We were aiming for £100,000 extra sales on pies. She showed me, with her computer, how £100,000 worth of bread sales instead would be worth an extra 18.7 per cent (the difference between the two contribution percentages), increasing the bottom line (I even used the phrase myself!) by £18,700. I confirmed that the salesmen's incentives could be directed towards bread without too much problem and that, pound for pound, the effect of marketing effort on turnover was much the same.

Appleby found it hard to argue with Chris and the evidence of the computer but did not give up easily. At the management meeting the next day, we had to approve the quarterly sales estimate and he started to argue for pies again. Jim was much in sympathy with his view that you can't leave a loss-maker so far below breakeven.

I tried hard to argue, using the ideas that Chris had rehearsed for me, but I was clearly on a loser.

"Jim," I said, "please could you ask Chris Goodhart to come in? She has all the data and she's worked out the profitability of the different product mixes."

"All right, Phil. Bring her in if she's available. She's more attractive than you lot. But only for a few minutes, we've got a long agenda."

Five minutes later Chris came in with her portable PC under her arm, looking as composed as ever, smiling confidently. Wasting no time, she explained the importance of splitting fixed and variable costs and how the direct/indirect split is all right for Universal's longer-term control but not for this type of tactical decision.

Then, cool as you like, she switched on her computer, sat next to Jim and showed him how we could make the extra £18,700 profit by selling bread instead of pies. Jim was completely bowled over, though I'm not sure whether it was by her or by the figures on the screen.

There was some token resistance. Appleby said it was inconceivable to leave pies as they were, losing money, and there were nods of agreement from one or two others. Chris replied sweetly that this was, admittedly, a central strategic issue which needed attention, though the indirect cost allocations needed checking to see how accurate they were. Maybe, she said, we would have to consider pulling out of pies altogether, a longer-term decision, but while they're still being sold, they give a contribution. Extra effort, however, was better directed to the higher margin bread products.

"Pulling out of pies is ridiculous," said Appleby. "We have to be in all three product groups – they're all integrated in production and customers expect all three."

"In that case," replied Chris confidently, "if you're in an integrated business, I can't see any point in producing separate calculations of net profit each month. We should concentrate on maximizing contribution of the company as a whole and that means selling the higher margin products."

Game, set and match.

Jim smiled as Chris left us and had great difficulty in returning to the agenda. After the meeting, he found it necessary to warn me about becoming involved with her, which I found very irritating. Of course our growing friendship and business relationship is nothing more than that, I keep telling myself.

Now it's nearly seven o'clock and I'm waiting for her because she's promised to give me the first of a series of tutorials on basic finance. I've ordered sandwiches and coffee so we can work through for a couple of hours. She's promised to show me the full projection of next year's budget including cash flow and balance sheet. I've always been just about able to understand profit and loss accounts, but the rest have been a closed book to me.

She comes, on time as always, computer under her arm. She plugs it in and I sit by her side at my table. She takes a disk and presses a few keys to load it. I soon see a profit and loss account on the screen, using the same structure as the one she used so tellingly at the management meeting. "Have we given up the old format altogether then?" I ask.

"Not necessarily. Universal will always want it and it may be continued in certain reports but, as with the quarterly product mix decision, I want to show you the effect of changes

Year's profit and loss account (£'000)

Sales	106,250
Variable costs	
Materials	41,260
Labour	15,600
Energy	4,040
Repairs	2,180
Distribution	6,500
Consumables	920
Commission	2,640
Total variable costs	73,140
Contribution	33,110
Fixed production costs	8,500
Profit before fixed indirects	24,610
Fixed indirects	
Administration	6,870
Research and development	1,120
Sales	3,470
Marketing	3,440
Personnel and training	780
Others	2,940
Total fixed indirects	22,620
Profit before tax	1,990

and that's where the fixed/variable split is so powerful."

"What are these figures exactly?"

"They're my estimates of the latest position this year," she tells me, "and they make pretty poor reading."

"Why? We'll make a profit of nearly two million and that's more than last year by about 20 per cent."

"I see we've got a lot to talk about. Aren't you concerned at the low margin, less than 2 per cent, which is down on last year?"

"Yes, but we agreed to hold prices to increase volume and it's worked. The bottom line is better." I was rather proud to be using this phrase again with confidence and to be making what I thought was a telling point.

"But what about the effect on return on capital and on cash flow?" she asks. "We've been pumping in extra investment to produce this higher profit and I'm not sure it's been worth it. Let me show you the balance sheet for last year and my estimate for this."

"I'm not sure I can cope with a balance sheet, Chris. It's always been a mystery to me."

"Nonsense," she responds abruptly, "you've been taken in by accountant's mystique. I'll just put the assets side on the screen and we can forget the other part – I'll deal with that some other time." She presses a few more keys.

Balance sheet (£'000)

	Last year	This year (latest estimate)
Fixed assets		
Property	1,628	1,628
Plant and equipment	8,499	12,201
Vehicles	2,462	2,999
Total (a)	12,589	16,828
Current assets		
Stock	10,628	13,806
Debtors	13,335	16,605
Cash	341	140
Total (b)	24,304	30,551
Total assets (a)+(b)	36,893	47,379
Less		
Current liabilities		
Creditors	9,682	10,280
Tax	740	881
Total (c)	10,422	11,161
Net assets (a)+(b)−(c)	26,471	36,218

I stare blankly at the screen. "This means nothing to me. What does it represent?"

"It represents the assets owned by Lawrensons at the end of each year. And the increases from last year represent cash pumped into the business by Universal on which we need to make a return. You said this year's profit is 20 per cent up on last year?"

"Yes, we made almost exactly £1.6 million."

She produces her calculator. "OK, £1,600 on capital employed of £26,471 gives a return on capital of 6 per cent. This year it will be £1,990 on £36,218 which is 5.5 per cent. Would you be happy with that if it was your business, your assets and your cash being pumped in?"

I try to grasp the significance of what she's saying and relate it to what Jim was telling us at an earlier management meeting: that our return on assets is far lower than Universal expects and that, despite our own pleasure at increasing profits compared to plan, Prior was still complaining that Universal's money would be better employed in the bank, without the hassle and the risk.

"Just tell me again what return on capital is, Chris," I ask. "Or is it return on assets?"

"They're both the same more or less," she explains. "Some call it ROI, return on investment, and many companies have their own special term. But they all measure the same thing. How good are the management at generating trading profit on the net assets which they use to run their business and which have to be financed from shareholders or from borrowing? It's generally accepted as the main measure of performance at the operating level."

"What do you mean 'at the operating level'?"

"Well, not taking things like tax into account. You could obviously take profit after tax if you wanted to measure management in the total sense."

"OK, I think I get the picture. What do we do now?"

"I'm going to work out a projection of next year's results which will show you the effect on return on capital and on cash flow of what we plan to do."

"How do you know what we plan to do next year?" I ask.

"You're going to tell me," she says, smiling, fingers poised on the keys.

Chapter 6

Here I am, gone seven o'clock learning about finance in the company of one of those boring accountants. Who would have believed it of me, the macho Sales and Marketing Director who, since his marriage broke down, has been spending his evenings chasing every bit of skirt in the vicinity? The staff at Lawrensons will never believe that finance is what I'm learning about, the accountant being an attractive woman alone with me in my office. But who cares?

I make an effort to avoid thinking of her as a woman and focus on the figures on the computer screen and the points she's been making. What she's saying seems more than logical – it's not just profit in money terms that is important, it's the return made on the assets invested in the business. I wonder why I've never seen it that way before?

"Come on, Phil," she says, "tell me your estimate of next year's sales with approximate price and volume increases. We can leave product mix for the time being as I'm only trying to illustrate general principles."

"All right but these are fairly broadly estimated figures. I would say about 3 per cent volume and a price increase on top of that. The price rises will partly be to pass on the extra costs of material and labour which Head Office are forecasting but I reckon the market will stand even more – about 5 per cent."

"You're sure about that level of price increase?" I nod

and she carries on putting figures into the computer.

"I've built the cost inflation increases into my calculations already," says Chris. "Five per cent on materials and 3 per cent on labour, though John Appleby says that the labour increase can be saved by productivity improvements. Let's see how it looks at the contribution level. My guess is that profit will be well up because price is so sensitive at the bottom line."

She presses some more keys and these figures appear on the screen.

Figures in £'000	This year	Budget
Sales	106,250	114,909
Variable costs		
Materials	41,260	44,623
Labour	15,600	16,068
Energy	4,040	4,577
Repairs	2,180	2,335
Distribution	6,500	6,962
Consumables	920	986
Commission	2,640	2,855
Total	73,140	78,406
Contribution	33,110	36,503

I'm becoming fascinated by the way the figures appear and I get a bit carried away. "Over £36 million contribution!" I shout. "More than £3 million up on last year! That's fantastic."

"We haven't actually made it yet, Phil," she reminds me, rather patronizingly I think, "and it's based on a lot of assumptions. Also, there'll be some increases in fixed costs which will begin to eat into the £3 million."

"But surely the fixed costs will be the same – that's what you told me last time we met. They're the same in money terms whatever the volume."

"Yes, but they're affected by inflation like other costs and some of them, like advertising, training, research and development, are discretionary."

"What do you mean by discretionary?"

She gives me a withering look. "It means what it says, Phil – at management's discretion. You can, in the short term, decide on spending levels and directly affect your short-term profit position."

Thinking about this, I recognize that these discretionary costs could make profit levels misleading as an indicator of one year's performance because management might cut them back and increase profits in the short term at the expense of the long. I store this away to discuss with Chris some other time.

I try to see on the screen how the extra £3 million has been earned. Obviously it's mainly the sales increase, which looks a hell of a lot – over £8.5 million.

"Could you just tell me how you arrive at your figures, Chris? The sales increase seems a lot and I can't quite see where your various cost increases have come from."

"OK, let's go through them one at a time. It's all based on formulae stored in the computer, but I can take you through it."

She moves over and I sit by her side, peering at the tiny figures on the screen. I wish I'd brought my glasses which I usually only use at home, but then I'm not sure my vanity would allow me to wear them with Chris there. Though, of course, she's only a professional colleague. Why do I have to keep telling myself that?

She resumes talking in her businesslike way, indicating each figure on the screen with the pencil in her hand.

"Sales are £106,250 plus 3 per cent for volume and 5 per cent for price. That gives you your £114,909. Materials is fairly straightforward, + 3 per cent because it's variable and the 5 per cent price increase which Head Office are forecasting. OK so far?"

"Hang on a minute," I say. "My poor sales and marketing brain doesn't work at the speed of yours."

I think of what she's saying about variable costs. They move with volume, so the total cost will increase by 3 per cent if the quantity sold goes up by that amount. And then the price increase will push up the amount spent by a further 5 per cent.

"Right," I say, "I'm happy. Can I trust the computer's arithmetic?"

Another withering look. "Here's a calculator, Phil, you could check the computer for me."

I ignore the sarcasm and, for my own satisfaction, enter in this year's material cost of 41,260, multiply by 1.03 and then by 1.05 to get 44,622.69. I tell her that her computer is inaccurate by 31p and we laugh together. Her smile is the nicest thing about her. I'd like to see her laugh more, outside Lawrensons. But then I remember my promise to Jim and to myself not to mix my business and personal lives again. We turn back to the computer screen.

"OK," she says yet again, "now you know that computers can round calculations off to the nearest pound. Now – what next – labour up by just 3 per cent."

"Now that must be wrong," I say. "You told me that Appleby would absorb the wage increase."

"Yes, he will, but this is the 3 per cent volume increase. Remember labour is a variable cost in our factory."

Thinking about this, I see that she's right. How could I have been so stupid as not to see it? At last I'm beginning to understand what a variable cost really means. We move on to energy.

"Energy costs go up by 3 per cent because of volume and I've put in a 10 per cent price increase because of the forecasts of oil and electricity prices. For repairs, distribution and consumables, I've put in a 4 per cent price increase, which is the likely general inflation figure I'm taking unless there is other special information. And of course they've been increased for the 3 per cent volume too."

"What about commission?" I ask. "That seems to have gone up by more than the 3 per cent volume."

"You're right, Phil." She looks at me with surprise. "I think you're beginning to break down your mental block about finance. You really are quite numerate – if only you'd forget that it's accounting and just think about numbers.

How do you think I've programmed the computer to work out the commission?"

I curse myself for not seeing immediately why commission will rise more than 3 per cent. Obviously it will move directly with sales, reflecting both the 3 per cent volume and the 5 per cent price increase. This makes me wonder about our commission system. Should we be paying a percentage on sales or should we gear it to volume? As things are, our salesmen stand to gain directly from price increases which may not always be the same percentage as the wage rises which other staff get. Something to raise with Chris, but not just now, I decide – another issue to store away. Looking at the figures like this is showing me many things in a different light.

"OK, Phil, so the contribution is £36,503 instead of £33,110 and you can now see the calculations behind the increase. Can I move on to fixed costs?"

"No, Chris, I'm still not sure why contribution has increased so much. From £33,110 to £36,503, that's an increase of over 10 per cent."

"10.25 per cent actually."

"All right, but why? Prices only increased 5 per cent and the costs all went up to some extent."

"Not labour. That was held – the only increase was for volume. The point is that the bottom line is very sensitive to price rises which are not matched by cost increases. We've put 5 per cent on prices, thus gaining over 5 million, and the increases on several of the costs are below that percentage. Thus the cumulative effect is bound to be significant at the contribution level. The increase of nearly £3.5 million is likely to be a high percentage increase on the base of this year's contribution – it would obviously seem less if it was expressed on sales or total costs."

I understand what she's saying and decide to catch her out. It also gives me a chance to use what is now my favourite phrase – the bottom line. I always think of Chris when I use it – I wonder if a psychologist would suggest a Freudian connection?

"You said the bottom line was net profit when we last met. Now you're using it to describe contribution."

"OK, Phil, you win. You're quite right – we accountants do tend to use these phrases rather loosely. But remember that the £3.5 million increase will go down to the bottom line if fixed costs are held at the same level, so in that sense it's valid."

We turn now to fixed costs and I notice it's after 8 o'clock. I suggest that we have our sandwiches and coffee before we carry on.

We sit at my table and I try to find out more about her.

"Do you have many interests outside work, Chris?" I ask.

"Yes, I've tried to develop as many as possible since I qualified. Passing accountancy exams tends to restrict your social life. I like the theatre and the opera. I belong to our local gliding club and would like to buy my own glider when I can afford it. And I like watching cricket when I've got time – it takes so much of the weekend, that's the problem."

"Who takes you to the cricket?"

I get the aggressive look.

"It is possible for a woman to go to a cricket match on her own, you know. Sometimes I go with my father or brother, sometimes with a friend, sometimes on my own. Is the next question do I have a regular boyfriend?"

"I must admit I'm curious."

"Well, I have no regular boyfriend and I don't really want one at this stage, so please don't get any ideas of that kind."

"That's not fair, Chris. I'm sure you've heard lots of stories about my behaviour since my marriage broke up and some are true. But I wasn't thinking in those terms, honestly."

"OK, I'm sorry. But there are rumours about us already and I'm not pleased about that at all. Though I suppose it's not your fault."

There's an awkward silence which she breaks by saying, "Phil, I'd like us to be friends. Tell me about your marriage."

I think about it. Why shouldn't I tell her? It can do no harm and it might do me good to talk about it.

"It was my fault mainly. Working long hours here. Using home as a lodging place. Not thinking of Jean and the children, growing further and further apart from them. Lots of rows, two stubborn personalities. The classic break up and we all lost – particularly the children. Looking back I just can't see how it could have happened. It was partly this place. It became an obsession, particularly before the takeover by Universal. I suppose I was your classic workaholic."

"Do you still see the children?"

"Yes, every other weekend. But it's difficult, though we usually manage to have a good time on the surface."

"And how do you get on with your wife?"

"Not well. She's still very bitter and we hardly ever speak when I collect the children. That's what hurts more than anything else. Once or twice she seemed to be getting more approachable but next time she'd cut me dead."

We chat on as we finish the sandwiches and coffee. It's wonderful to talk to someone and she's a good listener. I've not discussed my marriage like this with anyone for a long time.

It should seem incongruous to move from discussing one's broken marriage to working out next year's budget, but with Chris it seems quite natural. I move back to the computer with her, quite relieved that she's made it clear I can forget any idea of an affair. Even though I've been telling myself it isn't on, I know I wouldn't have needed much encouragement to change my mind.

"OK, where were we? Yes, fixed costs. John Appleby told me he will hold his costs at the same level next year. You have to admit that he's pretty efficient in that area, Phil. I'm putting administration and others in at the 4 per cent inflation level. You should know about sales and marketing. Any increases beyond inflation?"

"We'll have two extra salesmen in the London area, say £40,000 without commission, and I'm putting in for an extra TV advertising campaign pre-Christmas, about £75,000."

"Fine, what do you think about research and development?"

"Jim likes to keep it at a fairly stable proportion of sales, so I'd leave it at the same percentage as this year."

"Personnel and training? Shall I just put the 4 per cent on?"

I agree to this and she presses a few more keys.

The following appears on the screen below the contribution level:

	This year	Budget
Contribution	33,110	36,503
Fixed production costs	8,500	8,500
Profit before fixed indirects	24,610	28,003
Fixed indirects		
Administration	6,870	7,145
Research and development	1,120	1,211
Sales	7,470	7,809
Marketing	3,440	3,653
Personnel and training	780	811
Others	2,940	3,058
Total	22,620	23,687
Profit before tax	1,990	4,316

I can't believe what I'm seeing. Profits more than doubled?
That can't be right.

"Your computer must be wrong this time, Chris," I say.

"No, Phil. If your assumptions about volume and price
are right, that is what the profit will be. As I said before,
you're increasing price by 5 per cent while inflation is generally less than that so the effect is bound to be increased
profit."

"Yes, but the sheer scale of it."

"I know. Price is one of the most sensitive assumptions
so we must check it carefully. That's what sensitivity analysis
is for."

"What's sensitivity analysis?"

"Just asking 'What if?' questions and using the computer
to evaluate the effect. Now, tell me when you last increased
prices."

"Apart from the odd change for individual products, it
was about twelve months ago."

"And when will you bring next year's increase into effect?"

"From 1 April, in line with the TV advertising campaign."

"You mean, for the first three months of the year we'll

be working at the old prices while cost inflation carries on?"

"Yes."

"You might have mentioned that before. It will have a big impact on profit. Here, you input the revised figures."

She tells me that she's going to assume an even spread of volume over the year. She shows me how to amend the sales price increase from 5 per cent to 3.75 per cent (5 per cent for three quarters of the year). It's quite amazing how one quarter's delay in putting up price can have such an effect on profit. The summary on the screen shows:

	This year	Budget
Sales	106,250	113,541
Variable costs	73,140	78,372*
Contribution	33,110	35,169
Production costs	8,500	8,500
Profit before fixed indirects	24,610	23,687
Fixed indirects	22,620	23,687
Profit	1,990	2,982

*Commission down by 34 on lower sales

I whistle softly to myself. I'm beginning to see what she means by sensitivity. I start to see my pricing decisions in a different light.

"You see, Phil," says Chris, "that's why I want you and the others to work with me like this. Because, when you have the computer to do the number crunching, you can look at the effect of each decision before you take it. Thus you can see how the timing of your price increase is critical to next year's profit."

"Yes. I must think about that and how it will affect each product group. Your calculations assume 10 per cent increase all round from 1 April?"

"Right. It's a very simplified model to illustrate some basic points to you. When we prepare the actual budget, I shall need to do it in much more detail, looking at the seasonal sales pattern and each product line by line."

"Yes," I reply, "and I shall look at the timing again. I

think it will have to be 1 April, not just because of the TV campaign but also because I'm linking it to the new payment terms for customers."

"What do you mean by that, Phil?" asks Chris.

"Well, we're hoping to move to 45 days' credit compared to our present 30 because all our main competitors are offering longer than us and the big multiple chains insist upon it."

"You might have told me," says Chris, turning to her computer.

"Why, will it affect our profit?"

"Not directly, but it will affect our cash flow and capital employed. It might make it difficult for us to achieve an improved return on capital, even with the increased profit we've calculated. But it gives me a good chance to tell you about cash flow."

She looks at her watch and I do too. It's 9 pm. "We'd better call it a day," I say. "We can carry on next week. Let me buy you a drink."

I'm pleased and slightly surprised when she agrees. But immediately we enter the local pub – where many of Lawrensons staff hang out – I wish we hadn't come. A number of staff are there and, as we sit down in a corner, I see (or maybe imagine) them whispering about us. Then I see something I definitely don't like seeing – Jean with one of the secretaries she was friendly with when we were married and two men I've never seen before. I feel a totally unjustified sense of anger and jealously and Chris, seeing the look on my face, asks me what's wrong. When I tell her she looks at me sympathetically.

"Let's finish our drinks quickly and go, Phil. We shouldn't really have come here. I'd like to go home anyway."

I hope we can leave before Jean sees me but her eyes meet mine as I go out. I'm not sure what her look is meant to convey – maybe a mixture of contempt and triumph? But it makes it clear that I can forget those wild hopes of a reconciliation which have been stirring in me these last few weeks.

Chapter 7

Life for the single man can be depressing. The bachelor flat, so glamorous when there are women in your life, becomes lonely and cold when there aren't.

I spend the next weekend on my own because it's not my turn to have the kids. I go into the office on Saturday to write a plan for our next marketing campaign. At least I'm getting some pleasure and fulfilment out of my job now that Jim and Chris have helped me to see new direction in my career.

The rest of the weekend drags and I'm glad to get back to work and some company. During Monday and Tuesday I start looking forward to Wednesday evening with Chris, not just because I'm learning so much about the financial side of business but because I enjoy her company very much, however platonic our relationship is destined to be. She's promised to explain cash flow to me this time. I never understand the cash flow statements I get from Accounts and I'm hoping she'll make sense of them for me. I make it clear to her as we start that she should take it slowly and that I'll need a lot of help to understand the concept.

"Honestly, Phil," she says, shaking her head despairingly, "you have been conditioned by all this accounting jargon. Cash flow is the simplest thing of all – money, the bank account, the cash we put in and the cash we pay out. That's all."

"But it's not. The cash flow statement I get each month

has all sorts of things I don't understand – operating cash flow, sources, applications, movement in net liquid funds – it's all gobbledegook to me."

"Oh, I see your problem. That's cash flow calculated by another method which I'll show you later on. Now I'm just going to concentrate on cash flow as you know it in your personal life. The cash which comes in and goes out via your bank account, OK?"

She presses a few keys on her computer and continues her explanation.

"Now I'm going to go through Lawrensons' cash flow for next year based on a number of assumptions. Again I'm taking some rough estimates which will be refined when we finally do the budget. I'm leaving out the question of monthly phasing, just concentrating on the total year to show you the principles. OK?"

I nod, feeling more than ever like a little boy with his favourite teacher, but very appreciative of her simple way of putting things. Cash flow is just the bank account move- ment – simple when you see it in those terms.

"Right, Phil, what would you expect to see in the 'cash in' column for next year?"

"Well, we have the sales from the budgeted profit and loss account which we prepared last week. With the adjust- ment for the price increase from April, it was £113,000 and something."

"Right, but that's not cash is it? That's just the invoiced sales. How do we need to adjust it?"

"Oh yes, of course," I reply, "there's the adjustment for creditors, particularly with me giving more credit to customers next year."

"But it's not *creditors*, Phil. It's *debtors*. Debtors are your customers who owe you money. Creditors are your suppliers whom you owe money to. I know it seems the wrong way round but that's the way it is. I personally prefer the American terms – receivables for debtors and payables for creditors – they seem to describe them much better."

I agree. Why do accountants make life so difficult by their use of so many different terms?

"Now," she carries on, "what will be your debtors at the

end of this year? The figure we used in the balance sheet the other week was £16,605, which represents 57 days' sales. Is that still right?"

"Nothing's happened to change things, but how do you get your 57 days? I don't recall you telling me that before."

"Well, the balance sheet we looked at before showed £16,605 debtors at the end of this year and the sales will be £106,250. Express 16,605 as a percentage of 106,250 and it's 15.6 per cent, or, multiplied by 365, 57 days. That's the average collection period which will be outstanding at the end of the year. Hasn't anyone calculated that for you before?"

I shake my head and she shakes hers in reply.

"Quite amazing," she says. "Here you are, Sales and Marketing Director of a leading company, and you don't even know how to calculate your debtors ratio, never mind monitor it. It's not your fault, Phil – it's just that no one's seen it as their job to explain it to you before. People like Berisford and Marshall have a lot to answer for."

"But I can't understand why it's 57 days," I say. "We only allow 30 days, even to big customers."

"Well, either it's a seasonal variation or you've got a lot who are taking longer to pay. Why don't you have a look at it tomorrow?"

"I shall."

"Now, your new policy will extend credit by 15 days, am I right, so will that 57 days extend to 72?"

"I suppose so. Though that assumes I can't do anything to bring the 57 days down."

"OK, let's assume the worst."

She presses the keys again. I'm amazed at her speed and competence as she enters the data. The screen soon shows:

Cash flow – next year's budget ('000)

Cash receivable	
Opening debtors	16,605
Sales invoiced	113,541
Total cash collectable	130,146
Less closing debtors	22,397
Cash receivable	107,749

She points at the screen.

"The 22,397 is 72 days based on the year's sales budget of 113,541. Thus 22,397 will not be collected until the following year, OK?"

"Yes. I see. So, though sales in the profit and loss account are 113,541, you only collect 107,749 in cash."

"Yes, 107,749 is the actual money coming into our bank account. OK?"

She must think I'm stupid – it's all quite simple really. I see now that I ought to have been monitoring the days debtors outstanding. I wonder how frequently I should ask for the information? But Chris has already moved on to the cash being paid out next year.

"Right – materials. Our figure in the profit and loss is 44,623. Do you think I should put that in as cash out?"

"No," I say, rather pleased with myself, "raw materials are purchased on credit so there will be an adjustment for creditors."

"Any other reason why the raw materials figure in the profit and loss account needs to be adjusted?"

I look blank so she carries on.

"The profit and loss figure is raw material *consumption*. What you've actually used to produce what you've actually sold. It does *not* include the purchases of raw materials which go into stock. And Appleby's told me that stocks will increase by about £1 million next year with the extra volume and a new policy of bulk buying certain specialist materials. So though we *use* 44,623 next year, we'll have to *buy* 45,623."

"How much credit do we take from our suppliers then?"

"Well, the creditors for raw materials in the latest balance sheet are £7 million. The other creditors in the balance sheet are things like PAYE owing and other purchases on credit, so we can forget those for the time being."

"Are we going to take more credit next year?" I ask.

"No, the number of days will remain the same but the volume of purchases will increase in the budget. Now let's have a look on the screen."

Opening creditors	7,000
Purchases	45,623
	52,623
Less closing creditors	7,604
Cash payable	45,019

"Where does the 7,604 come from?" I ask.

She looks at some papers by her side.

"The usual credit taken is two months and the £7 million is about that level on last year's purchases. So the computer's calculated two months of this year's purchases to be carried over as creditors to the following year."

"Two months is a hell of a long time to keep our suppliers waiting, Chris. I just don't see the point, we must lose on price."

"Possibly, but we reap the benefit in cash flow as you can see. When we come to the balance sheet, you'll see that it reduces capital employed and thus helps return on capital."

My mind begins to boggle at all these dimensions. I'm not sure that I completely understand all she's saying, but I think I'll leave things for the time being.

She hardly gives me chance to pause for breath before moving on to the rest of the cash flow.

"Now what else do I have to put in? What other cash shall we pay out next year?"

"Tax? Presumably the tax people have to be paid their share and that will be a lot in view of the projected increased profit."

"No. In fact tax is paid at least one year in arrears. We'll be paying off this year's tax in next year's cash flow so it's that figure in the balance sheet at the end of this year – £881,000."

She enters this figure:

Cash flow	
Cash receivable	107,749
Cash payable for raw materials	(45,019)
Tax payable	(881)
Net favourable balance	61,849

"That's looking good," I say. "Universal can't complain about that."

"We've hardly started yet, Phil. We haven't paid you your salary yet, for instance."

I look back at the profit and loss account and see what she means. We've only included raw materials. None of the other production costs, fixed and variable, have been included yet. Nor have the operating expenses. I tell her this.

"There's something else missing too." She sees my blank look and continues. "What about your capital expenditure for next year? Your company cars, your new vans, your plant and equipment. We have to pay for those in cash, don't we?"

"Aren't they in the profit and loss account?"

"No. They're *capital* items. Things that will last for more than this year. They go to the balance sheet as assets but you still have to pay the cash out."

Again I curse my stupidity, but the structure of the three financial statements is beginning to emerge more clearly in my mind. The profit and loss account measures trading performance and includes the period's sales and operating costs, whether or not represented by cash transactions. Cash flow is the actual cash being received and paid out to support the operations. And the balance sheet is a statement of long-term assets bought and owned at the end of the period. As this sinks in, Chris continues.

"You see, Phil, accounting principles are based on the difference between revenue expenditure, to run this year's operations, and capital expenditure on assets to keep for the future."

I nod but there is something stirring at the back of my mind.

"What about depreciation? Isn't that somehow part of all this?"

"Yes, you're right. It's a most important part and it affects this cash flow, as you will see. What do you think depreciation is?"

"Isn't it the money you set aside to replace assets?"

"That's not really an accurate description. It can have that effect, as you'll see later when we move on to look at the cash flow from another angle, but it's best at this stage to see it in its simplest form. It's just a book entry which spreads the expenditure on capital items over their expected life and ensures that each year's profit and loss account bears a share of the total amount. OK?"

I nod but not very convincingly. She walks over to the flipchart in the corner of my office. I try not to notice her slender legs as she leans over to my desk to pick up a pen. It's been three weeks since Maggie left and I'm feeling the strains of my enforced celibacy. I think I'd make a very poor monk. My frustration becomes worse as she takes off the jacket of her suit, revealing an elegant blouse. This time the return to thinking about finance is even more difficult. She's written down some figures on the flipchart and I fight to concentrate on them.

Machine	Depreciation	Balance sheet value
Bought for 10,000	Year 1 1,000	9,000
	Year 2 1,000	8,000
	Year 3 1,000	7,000
	Year 4 1,000	6,000
Assumed life – ten years	Year 5 1,000	5,000
	Year 6 1,000	4,000
	Year 7 1,000	3,000
	Year 8 1,000	2,000
Cash paid out now	Year 9 1,000	1,000
	Year 10 1,000	0
	All charged as costs in the profit and loss account	Shown each year in the balance sheet

"That's all it is, Phil. The profit and loss account is charged so that the costs of each year include an equal proportion of the original value and the balance sheet figure reduces each year as it is written off."

I realize that I can catch her out again.

"But the costs in the profit and loss account you showed

me last week didn't include depreciation," I point out smugly.

"They did, Phil, though you couldn't have been expected to know that. You can show depreciation as a separate figure in the profit and loss account but Universal require us to show it within the functional headings, depending on whether it's production, sales, administration or whatever. So what should I do when I include these costs in the cash flow?"

"Take depreciation out because it's a book figure," I reply. "But you'll have to include this year's capital expenditure, won't you?"

"Yes, of course. Let's have a look at the paper Berisford gave me about depreciation and at the capital figures from Appleby and Marshall. You gave your capital items to Marshall, didn't you?"

"Yes, it was only company cars. There's nothing else on the sales side."

"OK, here we are."

She tells me that depreciation in next year's cost budget is:

Production	£1,280
Administration	£ 762
Sales	£ 92
Others	£ 88
	£2,222

"That admin. figure seems very high," I venture.

"Yes, it's the computers. They're written off over periods of between three and five years while most of the production plant is taken at ten years."

How arbitrary it all is – who knows how long those machines will last in today's uncertain times? Profit measurement could be distorted if someone got it wrong, intentionally or otherwise.

"I've also got next year's provisional capital budget."

Land and buildings	£682
Plant and equipment	£3,647
Vehicles	£894
	£5,223

"That's a hell of a lot, Chris. Particularly plant and equipment. Appleby throwing money down the drain again."

"I think that's a bit unfair. You've already seen the savings he's making on costs. He really is brilliant at using the new technology to improve efficiency, but you have to invest to do so. But don't worry, I'll make sure I check the savings by DCF before he actually goes ahead."

"DCF? What's that? Yet another bit of accounting jargon?"

"It's a method of investment appraisal to show whether the pay-off justifies the outlay. I'll show you that another time. At this rate we could be doing these evening sessions for another year."

"Would you mind?"

"Perhaps not but, much as I want to help, I do have a lot I like to do in the evenings."

I remember what she said about the theatre, the opera and the gliding club. I think about my own interests – absolutely none. That's why I look forward to my Wednesday evenings. How can finance tutorials be the most exciting thing in my life?

Chris is pounding away on the keys again and asks me to come and have a look. The cash flow has some more entries now and shows a very different picture:

Cash in	107,749
Cash payable for raw materials	(45,019)
Tax payable	(881)
Variable costs	(32,749)
Production costs (ex depreciation)	(7,220)
Fixed indirects	
Administration (ex depreciation)	(6,383)
Research and development	(1,211)
Sales (ex depreciation)	(7,717)
Marketing	(3,653)
Personnel and training	(811)
Others (ex depreciation)	(2,970)
Capital expenditure	
Land and buildings	(682)
Plant and equipment	(3,647)
Vehicles	(894)
Net cash flow	(7,088)

I'm no longer feeling quite so thrown by the columns of figures, taking Chris's advice to see them as nothing more complex than my own bank statement.

I try to check where all the figures come from. The variable cost figure is the total less the materials, which have already been included under payments to creditors. She's taken depreciation away from all the functional costs to give a net figure of cash paid out. Then she's shown the payments of capital which have put the cash flow into the red. But I still can't understand why the deficit is so high.

"Chris," I say, "how come we're 7,088 in the red when we're profitable? The capital expenditure is only just over 5,000, so that can't be the only reason."

"A number of factors, Phil. The main reason is your proposal to give more credit and there's the stock increase too. It's quite worrying – Universal aren't going to be happy with yet another year's adverse cash flow."

"I don't understand why Universal should care. We're making profit and that's what Jim and Prior are always going on about."

"Yes, but the business has to have cash to survive. Some Universal companies have to generate cash and Lawrensons have been taking rather than giving for too many years. At some point Universal are going to ask when all this investment is going to pay off."

"Do you think I ought to review the debtors policy then?"

"Possibly. It depends how fundamental it is to your strategy and to your sales forecast, but you should certainly think carefully about it. And I want to look at our creditor policy to see if there's any further scope for taking longer to pay. I also need to check other creditors apart from raw materials, which I've assumed as unchanged at present. But do you feel now that you understand cash flow and how it's different from profit?"

I nod and we smile in mutual satisfaction at the progress I've made.

"You must think me stupid not to know all this," I say.

"Not at all. I never fail to be surprised at the depth of ignorance of finance and, the higher the level of manager, the worse it seems to be."

We decide to call it a day and to work on the balance sheet next time. As we walk out of the office, we go on talking about the lack of financial knowledge among senior management.

"It's partly a cultural problem," Chris says. "Our education system doesn't train those who enter industry in the fundamentals of business. In most European countries and the US, this kind of subject would have been taught as part of University training. You'll find that just about every manager in a German company would have some kind of business degree."

"That's all very well, blaming the British attitude to industry. That's a classic excuse. I reckon you accountants are to blame. You want to keep it all to yourselves."

Surprisingly she agrees.

"You're right. The accounting profession has nowhere near the same influence in these other countries. And the business training of the other managers makes them realize that a lot of the jargon and mystique is unnecessary and unjustified."

"Do you reckon that a manager who understands finance is likely to have an edge over others?"

"I do, Phil. And I think you have a flair for it. Which you'll need if you're ever going to be an MD in Universal."

We have reached the car park and are ready to separate to our own parking places. She drives a new Peugeot 205 GTI, just the image for her.

"What makes you think I want to be an MD, Chris?"

"I can see it in your eyes. You want Jim's job, don't you? I think you should get it and, if these sessions are going to help, it will be worthwhile to me."

As I drive home to another lonely night in the flat, I think what a remarkable girl she is. She really seems to care about me and my future with Universal. She's young enough to be my daughter but still I don't mind her making the sort of comments which would be patronizing from anyone else.

And she's right. I do want Jim's job. Very badly. With no family future, my main meaning in life has to be my career. Well, I can use the learning I've gained to good effect.

That'll ensure that everyone sees me as the obvious successor
when Jim retires in three years' time.

Chapter 8

Next day it's the fortnightly management meeting. Years ago I used to look forward to these, particularly when Jim's Dad was alive. Business was expanding, we were part of a team and, though he would sometimes rave at us, we respected him and went away from those meetings with our adrenalin flowing.

More recently I haven't looked forward to our meetings at all. It's not Jim's fault – he can't help not having the personality of his father – and, even if he had, the spectre of Universal hovering over us has changed the atmosphere completely. Prior rarely attends but he's there in spirit all the time – that's the problem.

We all gather in the board room at 8.00 as usual – a legacy from the old man's days when he always insisted on starting early. I used to think it was because he was one of those people who hardly needed any sleep and who sparkled in the morning. It was not so good for those like me who only get going after the fifth cup of coffee.

Jim's looking serious and preoccupied – he doesn't seem to want to talk. Appleby's there as usual and, before we start, he grabs me to ask about my latest sales forecasts. He never seems to think or talk about anything but work.

Apart from Appleby, Jim and me, there's George Dixon, the Personnel Director. About my age, he's a quiet sort of chap who doesn't say much at meetings unless he's asked and who always sees situations in terms of his own role.

I've never heard him once make a contribution which related to wider business issues and he's been on the board six years – since just before the Universal takeover.

There's also Wilf Woodward, who's called Development Director and is just coming up to retirement. Wilf's a technical man, long a favourite of the old man, who helped him develop the high quality products which first built up Lawrensons' reputation. He was Production Director until Universal put in Appleby and we then moved him sideways to look after research and new product development. If he feels any resentment at being pushed out of production he doesn't show it. He's just coasting now, waiting to pick up his pension, and he tends to keep quiet too.

Berisford, the Chief Accountant, is also there. His presence goes back to the days when he was Company Secretary, and he still takes the minutes, which are produced in an unnecessarily formal way. He also reports on the cash position and brings his cash book into the meeting even though much of the accounting is now done by computer.

Finally there's Mike Marshall, the Cost Accountant, who's been coming to meetings for about a year since Appleby suggested that we needed someone to comment on the financial implications of decisions, particularly in view of Berisford's old-fashioned view of the accounting role. I don't particularly like Marshall – too clever by half, rather like Appleby – but his presence has been useful quite often, I have to admit. I believe that Chris would be far better – she seems to think about the business much more broadly, understanding the sales and marketing implications as well as production. Marshall seems to think only of minimizing production costs.

I've been wondering if I should suggest to Jim that Chris might come to these meetings, but I'm afraid he might misunderstand. And, despite the good impression she made at the meeting last month, no one else has suggested it. Perhaps best to bide my time and not be seen to be pushing her cause too much.

As the meetings are made up at present, it's really Jim, Appleby and I who do most of the talking. The others tend to sit and listen, waiting to be called in when information is required. I think Jim likes it this way and so do I. It was even better before Appleby came on the scene – everyone knew then that if Jim and I agreed there was no point in arguing. Appleby certainly doesn't see it that way and seems to love to argue about everything, even when we all know he's on a loser. But Jim's pretty good at shutting him up when it's gone on long enough.

The meeting is routine – monthly profit reports, decisions about sick pay for a couple of long-term absentees, reports on a disciplinary case and a change to a product specification.

The final item on the agenda is budget assumptions, which we always discuss each year at the meeting before the budget begins to be prepared. The Universal cost inflation estimates, which Chris used in her preliminary calculations, are confirmed. I'm given agreement in principle to my plans for extra salesmen and TV advertising, but Jim makes it clear that this is subject to the budgeted profit being satisfactory.

"Oh, I think you'll find the profit will be OK," I say, "as long as you agree the price increase I'm proposing. We haven't yet agreed that assumption for the budget."

"What are you suggesting?" asks Appleby. "I don't see how you can propose a price increase until we've finished next year's cost forecasts. I'm hoping we can keep producton costs close to this year's levels."

This irritates me. "I really don't see why our price increase should be on a cost plus basis. I don't want accounting figures to tell me how to price."

"Phil's right, of course, John," says Jim. "We can be guided by cost but, if we can increase our margins without losing volume, we shouldn't miss the chance. How much do you think, Phil, and when?"

"Five per cent from 1 April, and I think I can still get some volume growth even with the price increase."

"I doubt if a small price increase like that will make much difference to profit, don't you agree, Mike?" says Appleby, looking at Mike Marshall, who nods predictably. A yes man if ever I saw one. Remembering my work with Chris last night, I decide to make a point.

"In fact price is very sensitive at the bottom line." I hope I sound more convincing than I feel. "I was working it out on the microcomputer last night and I think you'll be surprised how it will improve return on capital, as long as we watch our costs."

They all look at me in surprise and there's a silence. Jim's initial expression of surprise turns to interest. "Can you be more specific, Phil?"

"Not yet, Jim. Let's wait and see the figures when we've got the final estimates in, but I think the net margin will be well up."

"Partly because I'm holding costs," Appleby reminds us and I concede the point, remembering what Chris said about his good performance in that area.

We agree the price increase assumption and quickly complete the agenda. We're just getting up to leave when Jim asks us to stay.

"I've got something to announce," he says, "and, as it affects you all, I'm going to tell you while we're together. I'd like to have seen you all personally but it has to be done simultaneously."

We all sit tensely. I wonder why Jim hasn't confided in me first. He always has in the past.

"We're getting a Deputy Managing Director," says Jim. "He's being put in by Universal, who feel we need to strengthen our management team. I've argued against it but I'm afraid I've lost and I have to accept it. I'm also committed to making it work now we're going to have him."

I sit there dumbfounded. Just when I was beginning to think that Jim's job was within my grasp if I could sort myself out in the three years before he retires. I'm surprised and disappointed that he didn't tell me first. I suppose he couldn't bring himself to do it, knowing how I'd feel.

I hear Appleby asking a question. "What's his background, Jim?"

"He's from Universal's subsidiary in Hong Kong, an Englishman who did some sort of business degree in the States. He's been Financial Director over there so I assume he's an accountant." Knowing Universal, it had to be a financial man, I think to myself.

"What's his name?" I ask, as if it mattered. My voice comes out as a croak and the others look round at me.

"Martyn Ames," says Jim.

"How old is he?" asks Wilf. Wilf regards anyone under forty-five as wet behind the ears.

"Thirty-three."

As the meeting breaks up I try to talk to Jim but he tells me he's got another meeting. I arrange to see him after lunch.

"I'm very sorry, Phil," he says quietly as we part and that empty feeling in my stomach gets even worse. He's sorry – what about me? But I can't really blame Jim. He knows as well as everyone else that this man will be the next MD. How could I have been so stupid as to think I ever had a chance?

I want someone to talk to but there's nobody at work I can confide in. In the old days I'd have gone home to Jean and talked it through with her. When I see Chris passing in the corridor I remember what a good listener she is. I ask if I can see her and we go to her office. I tell her what's happened.

"I've heard of Ames," she says. "He has quite a reputation. It's fairly typical of what Universal do, so you shouldn't be too disappointed. They often put a potential successor in early, though three years is a long time before."

"I might as well give up any ideas of getting Jim's job," I say. "I suppose I was being pretty fanciful anyway."

"Not necessarily. There have been cases where the man put in hasn't got the job and is moved elsewhere. Some people say they do it to create competition where there's only one internal candidate."

My spirits lift but I wonder if she's just making this point to buck me up.

"Are you free this evening, Phil?" she asks. I'm slightly disappointed when she carries on, "I've got to work on till six and I wondered if you wanted to carry on with the budget calculation. I was thinking that we ought to do the balance sheet while the cash flow is still fresh in your mind."

I might as well take up her offer. It will stop me brooding at home. Though, however much I learn about finance, I'm not going to be able to compete with an accountant like this new chap, Ames. I make this point to Chris.

"Nonsense," she says. "Some of these chaps with high

reputations aren't all they're cracked up to be. And your stance can be as a sales and marketing man. You don't have to compete directly with him, just choose the right issues to make your points. And I'll be there to help."

I don't really believe all this but I'm grateful for her efforts to make me feel better. We agree to meet about 6.30.

My meeting with Jim is very unsatisfactory. He seems to regret not having confided in me but says he was under instructions from Prior. Maybe this gave him the excuse to shirk it. He assumes that Ames will be given the job and sympathizes with my position.

"You were just beginning to get sorted out, Phil," he says. "It's bad luck. I wish they could have waited and I really did argue against it. But we must make it work, Phil. You will co-operate, won't you?"

I agree that I will but not very convincingly to Jim or to myself. I leave his office with next to no motivation to work for the rest of the day and I spend my time shuffling paper around, achieving very little. It's difficult to concentrate on anything.

Our meeting is in Chris's office this time. She's already set up the figures on the computer. It's the same balance sheet as she had at our first session, the latest estimates of our results for this year:

Balance sheet

	This year (latest estimate)
Fixed assets	
Property	1,628
Plant & Equipment	12,201
Vehicles	2,999
Total (a)	16,828
Current assets	
Stock	13,806
Debtors	16,605
Cash	140
Total (b)	30,551

Balance sheet (*cont.*)

	This year (latest estimate)
Total Assets (a) + (b)	47,379
Less	
Current liabilities	
Creditors	10,280
Tax	881
Total (c)	11,161
Net Assets (a) + (b) − (c)	36,218

"OK," she says, "can you remember what the balance sheet tells you?"

I think back to what she told me two weeks ago.

"It's the assets we shall own at the end of the year less the short-term liabilities owing. It gives us the net assets employed on which we calculate return on capital. Right?"

"Right."

"Surely that's not all the balance sheet is?" I say. "It doesn't balance. There's no other side."

"That's true," says Chris, "but remember that, within Universal, Lawrensons don't have a separate financial structure so we can't arrive at the other side. And, for management control purposes, it's easier for managers just to focus on the assets they use in the business."

"I don't quite understand what you mean."

She seems pleased that I'm so frank about how little I understand. "Well, first I'd better tell you what the two sides mean though, as we don't usually put them side by side these days, it's better to think of them as two sections," she says. "One section, the assets, shows your tangible possessions. That's the easy bit. It's the second section that causes the confusion. It used to be called liabilities, though different words are used now. I like to call it the sources section because it tells you where the money has come from to fund the assets in the other section. Where do you think Universal get the funds to buy their assets?"

"From shareholders."

"Right. But how?"

"Shares, I suppose. The capital that they've invested."

"OK, but how else?"

My silence encourages her to carry on.

"They also leave profits in by not taking all the profits as dividend. That's the second shareholder source – retained profits or reserves – the profits which have been left in the business."

She moves over to her flipchart and writes up:

Share capital	10
Retained profits	90
Shareholders' equity	100

"You've left out reserves," I point out.

"No. Retained profits is just another phrase for reserves. I don't like using reserves as a term. It implies that it's cash in the bank when it's really the way in which, since the company was formed, the assets have been funded."

I digest this point and then notice the very small ratio of share capital to retained profits, only 10 per cent.

"Why is the share capital so small?" I ask.

"I've done it on roughly the same ratio as Universal. It's all dependent on their financial policy over the years. Universal have hardly added any new share capital since they went public just after the war. Hence retained profits have got bigger all the time as they have ploughed profits back."

"Is that a good thing?" I ask.

"Depends on the shareholders and what they want," she replies, "but most shareholders prefer to have some of their profit ploughed back to help capital growth. They usually prefer this to the alternative ways of increasing shareholder investment – putting in more capital themselves or allowing someone else in share the ownership."

"But why not borrow from the banks instead?"

"They do. I just haven't explained loan capital yet. It's

often because share capital isn't available and retained profits are not enough to finance the business on their own that companies turn to loan capital. And gearing does have other advantages, as I'll show you some other time."

"Gearing? I've heard of that but I've forgotten what it means."

"It's just a term for the extent of loan capital in relation to shareholder's equity. I'll have to invent a ratio to show you the principles."

She writes on the flipchart:

Share capital	10
Retained profits	90
Shareholders' equity	100
Loan capital	100
Total sources	200

"That's sometimes called 50 per cent gearing," she says, "though some analysts and bankers would relate the loan capital to shareholders' equity and call it 1.0 or 100 per cent. It's the same thing in principle – just a different way of expressing it." Why can't accountants and bankers get together and agree a common terminology? Chris carries on before I can make this point.

"The gearing ratio is a measure of risk. The more you borrow rather than use your own money, the more vulnerable you are. Because the interest has to be paid whether or not a profit is made. It's just like you and me, the more we borrow, the more risky we are. The higher the gearing, the less secure the company, particularly if there are hard times ahead."

This seems straightforward. I wonder why I always thought gearing was some advanced concept? I'm highly geared if I have a big mortgage. If I save to buy the house myself, I'm more secure even though I don't have a very big house!

"Now," she says, "as Lawrensons haven't got a sources section to their balance sheet, I'm going to take the proportions I've used already and apply them to Lawrensons just to show you the effect. OK?"

I nod and she writes on another page.

Lawrensons net assets	36,218
Assumed sources	
Share capital	1,811
Retained profits	16,298
Shareholders' equity	18,109
Loan capital	18,109
Total sources	36,218

"Is that gearing ratio high, Chris?"

"It's fairly high by the standards of many companies. But it depends on lots of factors – profit levels, industry, degree of risk – I'll discuss this later, I promise. But I'd like to show you how Lawrensons' balance sheet will look next year if we work to the profit and loss account and cash flow we've already prepared. Let's examine the fixed assets first."

She puts some entries into the computer. The screen shows:

Fixed assets	Opening balances	+ additions	− depreciation	Net book value
Property	1,628	682	30	2,280
Plant & equipment	12,201	3,647	1,710	14,138
Vehicles	2,999	894	482	3,411
	16,828	+ 5,223	− 2,222	19,829

"How did you get all those figures so quickly?" I ask.

"I didn't put them all in," she replies. "We had the opening balance sheet figures in already and the additions were in the computer from the cash flow we did yesterday. All I did was to split the depreciation between the three asset headings. We used the total of £2,222 yesterday. The computer has formulae which automatically transfer from one document to another."

I look at the figures to see how the new balance sheet has been calculated. The opening values plus new additions, less depreciation charged for the year. I ask Chris why property depreciation is so small.

"Well, property often appreciates, doesn't it? In fact the accounting convention, which not all of us agree with, is not to depreciate land and to depreciate buildings over a long period. Universal take forty years, which is fairly typical. Though with some buildings which are really there for ever, even this seems unnecessary. But the accounting bodies like to have a standard and they ask for all buildings to be written down. Can we do current assets now?"

I agree and her fingers move over the keys again:

Current assets	This year (latest)	Budget
Stock	13,806	14,806
Debtors	16,605	22,397
Cash	140	(6,948)
	30,551	30,255

"Do you remember those figures, Phil?"

I remember the debtors from the previous day. The amounts still owing from customers at the end of the year – it's an asset because we have a right to collect that money in the future. And I recall that Appleby was forecasting a stock increase of a million pounds and we built the extra purchases into the cash flow. But the cash figure of a negative 6,948 is a complete mystery to me and I tell Chris so.

"Yes, I ought to re-program it to show in current liabilities. That's where an overdraft usually goes."

"An overdraft. Surely we can't have one, can we?"

"No. In practice Universal put in the extra cash flow. This is the balance sheet as it would be if we were independent."

"But how do we manage to be 6,948 in the red?"

"Simple. You remember we had an adverse cash flow of 7,088 yesterday? Well, we have 140 cash at the beginning of the year. That's the amounts we hold in floats and current accounts. So, if 7,088 goes out, we're left with a deficit of 6,948."

It dawns on me that the figures we looked at in the cash flow were more than accounting entries. They were estimates of real money. And if we weren't part of Universal, we'd either have to get an overdraft or go bust. I begin to see the full significance of my plans to increase debtors. One look at the balance sheet tells me how the increase in debtors accounts for much of the deficit. I mention this point to Chris.

"I'm glad you noticed that. A bit later on I want to show you a statement which highlights the balance sheet differences, but now I'd like to press on to current liabilities. I'll show fixed and current assets as summaries."

On the screen appears the following:

		This year (latest)		Budget
Fixed assets (total)		16,828		19,829
Current assets (total)		30,551		30,255
Total assets		47,379		50,084
Less current liabilities				
Creditors	10,280		10,884	
Tax	881	11,161	1,044	11,928
Net assets		36,218		38,156

"I don't recognize either of those two current liabilities figures, Chris," I say. "Creditors were seven million and something, weren't they, and the tax was nothing like that."

She consults her papers.

"Yes, you're right. Creditors went up from 7,000 to 7,604, an increase of 604, but that was creditors for raw materials only. There are other creditors for odds and sods like PAYE and National Insurance – don't you remember me mentioning them to you yesterday? I've assumed they won't change – the difference between the two is as we calculated yesterday, 604, isn't it?"

I see that she's right but I still can't reconcile the tax figure. I remember we assumed that 881 would be paid in the cash flow but can't understand the 1,044.

"No, I wouldn't expect you to, Phil. Let me move you back to the profit and loss account, then you'll see it."

She presses a button called 'window' and the profit and loss account appears:

	This year	Budget
Sales	106,250	113,541
Variable costs	73,140	78,372
Contribution	33,110	35,169
Production costs	8,500	8,500
Profit before fixed indirects	24,610	26,669
Fixed indirects	22,620	23,687
Profit before tax	1,990	2,982
Tax provision	881	1,044
Profit after tax	1,109	1,938

"I didn't show you tax before. We only went down as far as profit before tax. The forecast corporate tax rate for next year is 35 per cent of 2,982. You can see that the rate's quite a bit down on last year after the changes in the Chancellor's last budget."

"Why does that appear in the balance sheet though? It's already in the profit and loss."

"Because we'll still owe it at the end of the year," she explains patiently. "These are current liabilities, remember. Now, while we're on profit and loss, can you tell me the retained profit for the year?"

"That will be the same as last year, won't it?"

"No, remember it's a cumulative figure. We need to add the extra amount retained for this year. There's no dividend payable or, at least, we can assume that."

I realize what she means.

"It's the profit after tax then," I say, quite proud of myself though it really should been obvious, "1,938 will all be retained."

"That's right. So now we can look at the other section of the balance sheet. I'm assuming share capital and loan capital to be unchanged, so it should balance."

	This year	Budget
Assets		
Fixed assets (total)	16,828	19,829
Current assets (total)	30,551	30,255
Total assets	47,379	50,084
Current liabilities (total)	11,161	11,928
Net assets	36,218	38,156
Sources		
Share capital	1,811	1,811
Retained profit	16,298	18,236
Shareholders' equity	18,109	20,047
Loan capital	18,109	18,109
	36,218	38,156

Retained profits have gone up by the profit after tax figure of 1,938. Share capital and loan capital haven't changed, though Chris reminds me that they could have done if the adverse cash flow were to be funded from either of those sources. I can see that it balances but I can't understand why. Maybe Chris is like all the other accountants – having some mysterious way of making it balance.

"Chris," I say. "I've got a rather fundamental problem. I can't understand why it balances."

"It balances because everything we've entered maintains

the balance we started with. Depreciation reduces retained profits via the profit and loss account and reduces fixed assets. Cash paid out on fixed assets increases assets but reduces cash. Costs paid in cash reduce profits and also reduce cash. Don't you see?"

I do see and I think of other movements. Purchases of materials increase stock and reduce cash. Sales on credit increase profits and increase debtors. It's all so simple once you get the idea. This is what double entry means, nothing to do with book-keeping really. Just a way of recording both sides of each transaction which a company carries out.

"You'll see this even more clearly when I do a funds flow with you, Phil," she says.

"A funds flow? What's that?"

"It's a way of classifying balance sheet movements. It's not that complex once you get the idea. Can you take any more or have you had enough? I'd like to press on while the figures are fresh in your mind – it's only 7.45."

It is suddenly frighteningly clear that there is nothing in the world I would rather do than stay, even if we were discussing Einstein's Theory of Relativity. I just want to be with Chris. There's no doubt about it, there's no point in kidding myself any longer. Some people would call it middle-age infatuation but I know the truth. I love the girl.

Chapter 9

We sit drinking our coffee. All the other office lights are out. It feels very quiet, almost eerie compared to the bustle of the daytime. I think about my feelings for Chris. The last thing I should do is to say anything to her until I've thought it all through. She's already made it clear that I should forget any romantic involvement, so there's no point in saying anything anyway. But how long can I go on without making it obvious?

She starts to talk about this new chap Ames and how he'll find it difficult coming into a new place, particularly one where there is an old family tradition and where change is resisted. I ask her if she's voicing some of her own frustrations.

"Yes. I suppose I do find you all a bit resistant to change. But I've only just started and I'm at a lower level than Ames. It will be interesting to see if he just sits back and watches for a while or tries to make a name for himself. When is he starting?"

"Not for three months apparently." I heard this from Jim at our lunchtime meeting. "He has to hand over to his successor in Hong Kong before he can come over. Jim said that he might visit us next month. He's coming over to look for a property."

It's rather pathetic for a supposedly mature senior manager but it hurts me deeply even to talk about Ames. I must try to become more rational about it by the time he starts, otherwise it will be obvious to everyone and no good for me or the company. But if I was sensible and mature I wouldn't have fallen for this girl who is young enough to be my daughter. Who's sitting here with me now, giving up her theatre, her opera and the rest of her private life to help me understand cash flow, or was it funds flow? Why is she prepared to do this? Is she just one of those good, unselfish people who like to help others or does she feel something too. I can live in hope but I suspect I'm clutching at straws. We put away our cups and plates and it's back to the computer.

"OK, Phil. Now, where were we?" She's so businesslike for such a young girl and it endears her to me even more. The fight to concentrate, always difficult, is now even harder than usual.

"Now we're going to look at cash flow a different way. Can you remember our budgeted cash flow deficit?"

"Yes, over seven million, wasn't it?"

"7,088 to be precise. Mainly because of your plans to increase debtors and, of course, our capital expenditure."

"Right, but I may look at debtors again."

"Good. But let's take the same assumptions for this exercise. I'm now going to produce a funds flow or source and application of funds statement. It may seem a bit confusing at first but stay with it and I think you'll find it helpful."

It's very likely I'll find it confusing but at least I'll listen patiently. This subject must be difficult if she's preparing me like this. Though, generally speaking, I've been surprised how simple and straightforward much of what she has explained so far has been.

She goes to the flipchart, pen in hand again, calm and confident. She obviously enjoys the teaching role and I certainly enjoy being taught. I wish I'd met her twenty years ago, not only because of my feelings for her but because I could have done my job so much better if I'd known about the financial concepts and their relationship to my actions.

She writes on the flipchart:

SOURCES	APPLICATIONS
Where from	Where to

"What we're doing is identifying the changes that take place in the company's financial position. We'll look mainly at balance sheet differences and classify them as sources or applications. Sources tell you where the funds for the period have come from, applications what they have been used for – OK?"

I nod but can't really pretend that I understand. She carries on.

"The starting point is profit for the year, which is a crucial source of funds. There are various levels of profit which you can take – we'll take the profit before tax of 2,982. Do you remember that figure?"

This was the profit figure after we adjusted for the delayed price increase and on which we calculated the tax provision. She writes on the flipchart:

Sources (where from)	
Profit before tax	2,982
Add back depreciation	2,222
Funds generated	5,204

"Before you say anything, Phil, I know it seems strange that depreciation is a source of funds."

"You can say that again. You told me yesterday that it was a book entry. You can't have it both ways. You're beginning to sound like all the other accountants."

She smiles and turns over to another page of the flipchart. I'm pleased that our relationship has developed to the stage where we can banter with each other. The atmosphere between us is very relaxed, considering we've known each other such a short while.

While I'm thinking about this, she's already telling me why she hasn't been misleadng me about depreciation.

"I know it sounds Irish but it is because it's a book entry that it's a source of funds. Forget our figures for the moment – think about a company with these sales and costs."

Sales	500
Costs	450
Profit	50

"You agree that profit is a source of funds?" I nod. "And that one of your costs is depreciation?" I nod again.

"Let's say that depreciation is 30 of the 450, OK? What is the amount of costs that are paid in cash, bearing in mind that depreciation is just a book entry?"

I begin to see what she's getting at.

"420," I reply.

"OK. Then let's look at the profit just in cash terms, assuming that there are no other changes in working capital – sales are for cash and other costs for cash."

She writes:

Sales (cash)	500
Costs (cash)	420
Funds generated	80

"The other way of arriving at that figure is to add back depreciation to profit. Fifty profit plus 30 depreciation gives us 80. It's really the profit before depreciation – as it would have been if none had been charged. It represents the funds ploughed back into the business before adjustment for other balance sheet changes."

"Is that phrase – funds generated – in general use?"

"There are a number of different terms used. That's a typical one and it's used in Universal. Some analysts call it cash flow, which I think is misleading because there are many other items which affect the final cash flow, as we saw yesterday. Let me show you how we deal with those. I'll need to bring up on the screen the balance sheets for this year and budget, so we can focus on the changes."

In almost no time the two balance sheets appear on the screen and I recall the way the figures have changed as a result of the next year's projections which we agreed.

Assets	This year (latest)	Budget
Fixed assets		
Property	1,628	2,280
Plant and equipment	12,201	14,138
Vehicles	2,999	3,411
Total	16,828	19,829
Current assets		
Stock	13,806	14,806
Debtors	16,605	22,397
Cash	140	(6,948)
Total	30,551	30,255
Total assets	47,379	50,084
Less current liabilities		
Creditors	10,280	10,884
Tax	881	1,044
Total	11,161	11,928
Net assets	36,218	38,156

"I've left out the other section of the balance sheet as the only change was for retained profit, which we've already taken. If there had been increased share or loan capital, this would have to be included as a source. But as we're part of Universal, we obviously don't raise our own capital."

This reminds me again how we are cushioned from the real world compared to the days before the takeover. It occurs to me that I would never have planned to extend credit terms without the old man's permission and he would have gone up the wall if it had increased our borrowing to this extent. He would have reminded me of the cost of the overdraft and asked me why we needed to finance our customers' businesses for them. Though customers are a lot more powerful these days, as I keep telling Jim.

Chris takes her place at the flipchart again. I think that, whatever happens to her and to us, I shall always remember her, pen in hand, eyes shining, showing the obvious pleasure she derives from helping others to understand her subject. If there were a few more accountants like her, there wouldn't be half the confusion that exists among poor non-accountants like me.

"OK, Phil, please concentrate," she says, evidently noticing the far-away look in my eye. I meekly accept her admonition and go back to concentrating on the sources and applications statement, wondering why she's paying so much attention to the balance sheet changes. Hadn't I already seen those as we built up the balance sheet?

"Now. Remember that sources show where from and applications where to. I'm now going to show you how the balance sheet movements fall into those categories. We've already got funds generated as a source, OK?"

She writes:

Sources (where from)		Applications (where to)
Profit before tax	2,982	
Add back depreciation	2,222	
Funds generated	5,204	
Increased liabilities		Increased assets
Reduced assets		Reduced liabilities

"Now I know this is difficult to grasp without figures, but can you see why they fall into these categories?"

"Yes, I think so," I say. "Increased liabilities as a source – like when you take extra credit from suppliers. And increased assets as an application, I can see that too. I'm not so sure about the reductions. Can you explain those to me?"

"OK. Well, a reduction of stock would provide a source of funds. Or if you reduce your debtors and collect extra money. Or even if you sell off fixed assets. They're all ways of raising money. And if you reduce your liabilities by paying your suppliers more quickly, that's an application – you're applying funds for that purpose."

"Right, I think I'm with you. But I'm not sure where it's all leading."

"I said you would only see it clearly when all the entries are made. Let me show you how it looks with some figures in."

This time it takes a bit longer for the computer to produce the figures., Chris tells me that she's had to adjust a formula on her spreadsheet. Eventually the screen shows:

Source and application of funds statement

Sources		Applications	
Profit before tax	2,982	Fixed assets purchased	5,223
Add back depreciation	2,222	Increased debtors	5,792
	____	Increased stocks	1,000
Funds generated	5,204	Tax paid	881
Increased creditors	604		
	5,808		12,896
		Adverse cash flow	− 7,088

After staring at this for a while I suddenly become aware of what it's telling me. It's showing how the decisions in the budget have affected the cash flow. How the funds generated from operations have been nearly enough to fund fixed assets, but the increases in stock and debtors have caused that adverse cash flow of over 7 million.

"Can you see it now, Phil?" says Chris, taking in my interest. "It's the other way of arriving at cash flow – by balance sheet differences. And it shows very neatly how your decisions affect cash flow."

"Like debtors, you mean," I say and we laugh together. "It certainly does show the effect of that decision very clearly. But where does that tax figure come from, the 881?"

"That's the tax paid. That must go in applications because we have the profit before tax in sources."

"But I thought it was 35 per cent of profit, over a million?"

"That was the tax provision in the profit and loss account. The cash flow is affected by the tax actually paid, even though it relates to the previous year."

I read through the statement again. It tells you a lot about the business in a very concise way, once you understand the structure behind it.

"I wish I'd seen one of these before," I say.

"You do actually see one each quarter. The operating cash flow statement for Universal, though I admit it's very complex and detailed – developed by accountants for accountants I'm afraid. If you like I could simplify it for the management meeting – do you think it would be helpful?"

"Yes, I do, I'll speak to Jim about it. Is there anything else you can pick up from this sort of statement?"

"I always like to see if the long-term sources more or less cover the long-term applications. This looks good because funds generated are only marginally short of fixed asset purchases, so the overdraft is mostly funding working capital, not long-term assets."

I remember that working capital is the phrase for current assets less current liabilities, mainly stock, debtors and creditors. At last the terminology seems to be coming to me more naturally.

"And I often use these statements before I calculate financial ratios. Any big change would lead you to look further at a particular aspect. If I were looking at these accounts as an analyst, I would instantly focus on the debtors ratio because the debtors movement stands out so much."

"What do you mean by debtors ratio?"

"Debtors in relation to sales, remember we looked at it yesterday. You were surprised it was as high as 57 days."

She must be wondering about my memory and mental capacity. But I'm gradually getting there.

"The other process they're good for," she continues, "is longer-term cash flow planning. It's fairly easy to project a five-year cash flow by this method, without going into all the detail of the cash position as we did yesterday. You can just look at broad asset differences."

"Are these statements produced by all companies?" I ask.

"They've become very common in the last few years.

They're part of the published accounts of quoted UK companies and they're becoming increasingly popular for management information purposes. The problem is that the accountants can't agree on a standard format and they often complicate them far too much."

I think I'm beginning to understand what she meant by a management accountant when we talked over lunch that first day. It's not so much the figures that are important but the way they are presented and how far they are useful to the managers who receive them. That's why she's so good at her job. She thinks about what I need and not the accounting technicalities. Perhaps I should tell her this? I feel too embarrassed. Anyway she's progressing to something else already. But I'm feeling pretty tired.

"I think I've had enough, Chris," I say. "Shall we call it a day?"

"I'd just like to work on the final return on capital figure, to see how the budget looks. It won't take long and it will round off what we've been doing. I'll just bring back the summary balance sheets and profit and loss accounts." They appear on the screen:

	This year	Budget
Profit and loss account		
Sales	106,250	113,541
Variable costs	73,140	78,372
Contribution	33,110	35,169
Production costs	8,500	8,500
Profit before fixed indirects	24,610	26,669
Fixed indirects	22,620	23,687
Profit	1,990	2,982
Balance sheet		
Fixed assets	16,828	19,829
Current assets	30,411	37,203
Total assets	47,239	57,032
Current liabilities	11,161	11,928
Net assets	36,078	45,104

The figures surprise me. I feel sure the budgeted net assets figure is more than we saw earlier on. When I mention this to Chris she smiles.

"The more I work with you the more I'm convinced that you're really quite numerate. You're right. Can you think why it is?"

I wonder but just have no idea. What other assets could we have bought? I admit defeat and ask her to tell me.

"It's the negative cash. Remember we had a cash figure of minus 6,948 which was reducing current assets. Universal ask us to take out cash when calculating capital employed. The reason's pretty obvious – why should we benefit from our negative cash position when assessing our return on capital? The money's gone into the assets we're using."

I see this point and notice that the cash figure for this year has also been taken out – the 140 which will be in the bank at the end of the year. I'm not quite sure why this should be adjusted so I ask her to explain.

"Well, we're only holding the 140 for convenience. Universal often ask us to keep a certain balance in our account to help reduce bank charges. But it's not part of trading assets, is it? And that's what return on capital is – trading profit on trading assets."

"OK," I agree, "let's work out the figures then."

"Well, you tell me which I take."

"I guess it's 1,990 on 36,078 and 2,982 on 45,104. The only thing that worries me is whether that's strictly correct."

"Why?"

"Well, you told me that the balance sheet shows the position at the end of the year, whereas the profit is throughout the year. It seems inconsistent."

"You're right, Phil. That really is an excellent point."

I feel like a little boy who's received a gold star from his teacher. She carries on.

"Many companies do take the average during the year, using quarterly or half-yearly figures. Universal just accept the occasional distortion and prefer to keep it simple, using end-year figures. It probably doesn't make much difference over the years."

"All right let's see how it looks anyway." I actually feel

quite excited about the results. I haven't felt this sense of anticipation since the Universal takeover – the old commitment really is coming back.

Chris presses a few buttons and we see:

	This year		Budget	
Profit	1,990		2,982	
Net assets	36,078	= 5.5%	45,104	= 6.6%

She looks disappointed.

"I was hoping for a bigger improvement," she says. "Universal are going to be looking for at least 10 per cent. They don't regard a company making less than 10 per cent as even contributing to the group. They could earn more by investing in the money markets."

"But we've improved profits by more than half," I say. "Even Prior can't complain about that."

"Well, he will and he should. And so should you. This company will never be secure in Universal until we're making enough money to justify the risk of their investment. They look for 20 per cent – that's the point where you've really made it in Universal."

"What do you suggest then?"

"We'll need to think about it again when we've got the detailed budget calculation. But we know that price is very sensitive, so you might look at the amount of the increase and the timing again. And your debtors, of course."

"But I thought they only affected cash flow."

"No, they're in capital employed too, aren't they? One of your current assets."

I see this point, again aware of the limitations of my rusty brain. I begin to think that the real problem has been lack of use. For years I haven't looked at figures with any interest and it's just beginning to come back. Perhaps Chris is right. I am fairly numerate if I can have regular practice and develop my confidence.

She picks up her papers, switches off the computer and we walk out to the lift. It's 9.30 pm.

"You know, Phil," she says in the lift, "if you were a woman friend and not a man, I'd invite you to my flat for a coffee. I always think it's a shame that a man and woman can't be friends without people getting the wrong idea. They'd be bound to assume the worst if I did ask you back."

"The worst?"

"Well, you know what I mean. They'd assume that we were having an affair."

"I might like that," I say and instantly regret it. My face goes hot and I feel sweat trickling down the side of my head.

She says nothing. We walk out of the building and into the car park in silence. How could I have been so stupid? I'd told myself that I must think the situation over carefully and now I've blown it. I sense her anger and disappointment as we walk along and I feel I have to say something.

"I'm sorry, Chris," I say rather feebly, "I was only joking."

"I know, Phil. But you must also know how I feel. I want us to be friends and that's all."

"Yes and I want that too. I really do appreciate all the time and help you're giving me. You're a very good friend and I need one at the moment."

She smiles and I know that my feelings for her are stronger than ever. I wonder if she can sense it.

"When's our next evening session?" I ask.

"I don't think we need any more. You've got the basic principles of financial structure now and everything else I want you to know about is in the area of management accounting. That's best explained as things happen in the business, so we'll have informal sessions as the occasion arises."

We say goodnight and walk to our cars. I sit in mine for about ten minutes without moving. Yes, I tell myself, you really have blown it. You and your big mouth. You've lost whatever chance you had of getting closer to her. Now she doesn't even want to see you for any more evening sessions. You've lost her and your chances of learning enough about finance to challenge Ames for the Managing Director's job.

Chapter 10

Next Monday morning I find, at the top of my in-tray, a memo from Chris. It reminds me that Universal have to have their budget figures in a month's time and we must put in our estimates within two weeks to give her time to put them together.

I notice Chris assumes she will co-ordinate the budgeting process. I wonder if she's checked this out with the others in Accounting, particularly Marshall and Berisford? In previous years, these two have done it as a joint effort with no one really taking control and managing the process. She must have it cleared – I hope so for her sake. But I'm pleased that she's going to be taking a leading role.

Of course I'm pleased – it gives me an excuse to work with her again. Since my gaffe on Thursday evening, I've felt quite depressed – the combined effect of the rebuff from Chris and my concern at the new Deputy MD's appointment.

Nevertheless the weekend was pleasant enough, at least by the standards of the last month or so. I took the kids out to the local leisure park and we had a good time, or as good as you can in the circumstances. Now I only see them every other weekend, we seem to be building new relationships all over again each time. And by the time we feel natural with each other, the day's over and it's time to take them back home. Jean was at the door as I dropped them off and we actually managed to have a civilized conversation, which surprised me after our encounter in the pub.

I also had a date on the Saturday evening. I decided I'd better start developing my social life and phoned a divorcee friend, a former pal of Jeans's. We had a mutually satisfying Saturday evening which fulfilled our physical needs but little else and I longed for the days when Jean and I spent our weekends together with the kids. They were happy, homely days – if only I'd known how precious they were at the time, but you don't realize until it's too late.

So it's back to the budget. Normally I would have regarded it as a horrible chore, particularly on a Monday morning, but an excuse to contact Chris again is quite a compensation.

I dislike producing budgets. It's become a bureaucratic, political process which starts with me filling in the forms only for Jim later to alter all my figures and assumptions. Last year I told him that he might as well produce the budget himself and let me know the figures later.

The problems started soon after the Universal takeover. The first year we produced a slightly optimistic budget, which had been our style before Universal came on the scene. The old man made us work to operating plans which stretched us.

We failed to achieve the budget target that first year and Jim was to learn something about Universal politics. The fact that the results were good by any standard didn't seem to matter, we had not delivered our "bottom line", which was a sacred commitment within Universal. It was made clear to Jim that he might get away with it once but after another shortfall he might as well prepare for early retirement or a posting to Universal's punishment ground – West Africa.

In the second year after acquisition we went the other way. Jim, thinking of that West African posting, told everyone to be conservative in their estimates – "belt and braces" was the message – and we ended up with about five belts and five pairs of braces as everyone up the line built in their own contingencies, reducing sales estimates and building in cost reserves.

After all that, it wasn't surprising that our budgeted profit was well below what Universal needed. I remember Jim coming back from his budget presentation to the Universal board after Prior had rejected the budgeted return on capital as inadequate. We then had to re-do the budget for a further presentation a few weeks later and Jim told us to put in figures at the levels which he expected Prior to accept.

This made us all demotivated and cynical and, though things settled down a bit in subsequent years, the main factor in deciding the level of sales, costs and profit is still what Jim thinks Prior is expecting as a return for Universal. This seems to vary from year to year according to the mood of the Universal board and the performance of other companies in our division. It's a million miles away from what I thought budgets were supposed to be and from the days before Universal took us over.

I give Chris a ring to fix a meeting to share my reservations about our budgeting process.

"I'm sorry, Mr. Moorley. She's preparing the budget forms and she's asked not to be disturbed except in emergencies," says Mary, the rather officious secretary whom Chris shares with Berisford.

Maybe Chris has left instructions that I'm not to be put through. I feel even more depressed. But then that feeling is replaced by annoyance. After all, I am Sales and Marketing Director and, even if she doesn't want to give up her evenings any more, she has a job to do and discussing the budget with a Director is part of that job. I call back. Mary's on the line again.

"This is Moorley," I say. "Please tell Miss Goodhart that I cannot start my budget estimates without seeing her so there's no point in her preparing the forms."

In a moment Chris is on the phone.

"Hello," she says.

"Hello," I reply, "it's Phil Moorley. You've been rather difficult to get hold of this morning."

"Yes, Phil. I'm sorry. Mary was being over-protective. She shouldn't have put you off. Well, what can I do for you? We haven't seen each other for a while, have we?"

She sounds quite bright and friendly so I wonder if I've been worrying unnecessarily. Perhaps our misunderstanding last Thursday has not made her unwilling to help me again. Maybe her reason for stopping our evening sessions was a genuine one. I decide on a rather more placatory approach than I had planned.

"Chris, I need to talk to you about the budget. I've got the forms and there are some issues we need to sort out before we start. And you need to know the history. Can we meet today some time?"

"Yes, I'd like to. We did agree that we'd discuss management accounting issues when they arise in practice, so this is our first chance, I'll come now if you're available."

"Fine," I say. "See you in five minutes."

This cheers me up a great deal. It seems that she was being genuine and she really does want to see me. Suddenly I'm thinking like a schoolboy on his first date. I must put my feelings aside and start behaving like the mature company director I'm supposed to be. I must treat her like any other work colleague.

As she enters my office, I find that this is easier said than done. She's so composed for someone of her age, so full of life that it makes me feel guilty about my own moods of depression and cynicism. She sits opposite me and looks at me with those penetrating eyes. I tell her about the history of our budgeting since the Universal takeover and she listens with keen interest. After I've finished she's silent for a while and I wait for her response. I expect her to be appalled by the way company politics and personalities have distorted our figures.

"This isn't quite what I anticipated, Phil," she says. "I've never quite realized before what a big influence Universal has on the way you budget in the operating companies. I've always assumed that the figures were reasonably fair and accurate. My management accounting training never said anything about the kind of distortions you've described. The theory is that the estimates should be as accurate and realistic as possible to provide good information for financial planning and for management control."

"That certainly doesn't happen here," I reply. "If the budgets are optimistic, no one uses them for control purposes because they don't believe in the original assumptions. If they're too pessimistic, people are patted on the back for achieving soft cost and sales levels."

"And we have unrealistic figures for cash and profit forecasts," Chris adds, looking concerned.

"And another problem is that no one really knows who is supposed to be involved in the budget. Should it go down to the level of my salesmen who are in touch with the customers, or should it be Jim's estimate applied on a top down basis? We never get this clear. I try to do it bottom up but he seems to have made up his mind already, based on what Universal are demanding as budgeted profit."

"I'd like to think a bit more about this," says Chris, getting up. "I see now that we must agree the objectives of the budgeting system – what we're trying to do and who we're producing the information for – you, me or Universal."

"Or all three?"

"Perhaps. I'll do some more work on this and probably have a word with one of the lecturers who helped me when I was qualifying. Can I see you tomorrow?"

I'm pleased to find an excuse to see her again and agree to meet in her office the next day.

Later that day Jim pops into my office for a chat. It doesn't happen so much these days, particularly since the new Deputy MD's appointment was announced. It hasn't been mentioned since and I suspect that he's still embarrassed about it.

We talk about this and that, rather as we did in the old days. We arrive, as usual, at Universal and the pressure which the company in general, and Prior in particular, puts on all of us. Jim mentions his dread of the usual argument which he will face in the forthcoming budget negotiations.

"Jim," I say, "the budget's nothing like it used to be in your old man's day. I just wonder what the objectives really are and why we bother?"

"Well, we have to do it for Universal and that's not much more work than it used to be in the old days. Dad used to insist on budgets before the year began."

"Yes, Jim, that was good and there used to be commitment, our commitment to him. And we used to agree realistic figures which were useful for control. Now it's all between you and Universal. The figures are practically useless for control because I don't feel I own them after you've negotiated with Prior. Remember when you added 5 per cent to my sales budget after the Universal presentation? We didn't achieve it and all my lads were cheesed off."

Jim stays silent for a while.

"I see your point, but what do we do about it? I've told you before that we're not going to change the way Universal behave."

"Yes, I know, Jim, and I'm not sure what we can do yet, but I'm trying to work something out with Chris."

"You're quite taken with her, aren't you, Phil? I know she's a bright girl and she's making quite an impact. But she's on dangerous ground here. You know Universal. Achieve your budgeted bottom line or you're on your bike. Anyway, must go, see you."

Next day after lunch, I go to Chris's office. She's writing on the flipchart by her desk – she's always using this way of communication with me and the other managers. She's drawn a diagram which reminds me of those I saw on a management course I once attended at Universal's training centre. Every day we had a new matrix. Chris's looks like this:

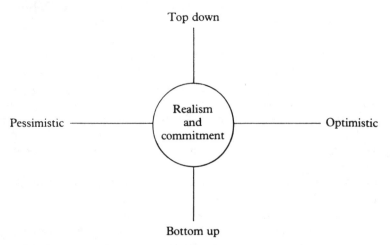

"Where on earth did you get that from, Chris?"

"I developed it after talking on the phone to that lecturer I mentioned. Don't you like it? Doesn't it sum up what we ought to be doing and where we are now?"

I look at it for a moment. I'm not sure what she's getting at but the framework begins to ring a few bells.

"Now," she says, "where were you on this matrix that second year after acquisition when you told me that Jim asked you to produce 'belt and braces' in your estimates?"

"Top left, I suppose. The Universal attitude to budgets, based on the fear of failure, caused us to budget pessimistically."

"Yet Universal insisted on more optimistic figures when the first budget was rejected. Did that mean that you ended up with realistic figures?"

"No. Even the adjusted budget was fairly pessimistic – we stayed in the top left."

"See how the framework helps you to think about it? What about the days before acquisition when Jim's father exerted the top down influence?"

"It was more like top right. He used the budget to stretch us all."

"But did you, in the end, feel committed to achieving budget performance levels?"

"Yes."

"Did you usually achieve them?"

"Yes."

"Were you able to negotiate with him?"

"Yes."

"Then I think he got it right – he was in the middle circle," she says. "I'm convinced that a good budget system achieves the middle of the matrix – realistic figures, but with some give and take from negotiation. They may be stretching but the important point is that you're committed to them in the end. That's what's missing with our present situation because we're confusing objectives. I wish it was as easy to solve the problem, though."

"What do you mean by confusing objectives, Chris?"

"Well, Jim's objective is to send Universal the figures he thinks he can get away with, so that he can maximize his own performance against budget. He'll try to budget pessimistically and Universal will try to pull him the other way. But you, I and all the other managers want realistic figures that we're committed to and which we can use later for control."

"Shouldn't Universal want realistic figures, too?"

"If they had any sense, yes. Not just for control purposes but for cash and profit forecasting, too. Yet when I think back to when I was working in Head Office, I'm sure that most divisions were playing the same game as Jim and the figures eventually agreed depended on how good they were at playing the game. In some operating companies they could end up in the top right corner because the MD is either too weak or too innocent to resist Universal's pressure to achieve high performance levels."

I look again at the matrix to see what she means by "top right". Top down, optimistic. Yes, I can see Prior doing this to someone not so experienced and wily as Jim.

"This is all very academic and interesting, Chris, but where does it leave us? We've got to start the budget soon."

"I'd like to come to this week's management meeting to raise it with Jim and the others. I've got a rather controversial suggestion that will need their commitment."

"I'll ask Jim. I should think he'll agree." I don't add that he'll be more likely to agree because of her attractiveness than because of his interest in the subject. "But tell me about your suggestion."

"OK, but please don't tell the others without me having a chance to explain. I'm going to suggest two budgets."

I try to communicate silently my horror at the idea of going through my least favourite financial process more than once.

"I can see I shouldn't have told you, Phil. I'll make the reason clear at the meeting and the preparation won't take as much time as you think. And, if we can get realistic budgets accepted by Universal, it won't be necessary anyway. I must go now – I'm meeting John."

I wonder who "John" is. Of course, she means Appleby. I remember she told me last week she was working with him to develop the management information in the factory. I feel a pang of jealousy which is quite unjustified. I'd secretly been hoping that Appleby's early lack of co-operation with Chris would continue. But she has to do her job and getting on with all the management team is part of that job. I wonder how Marshall feels about her being so closely involved in the budget. I ask Chris about his reaction.

"He tolerates me, just about," she smiles. "We're having our own little power struggle and he's particularly put out that I'm doing the budget. But that was agreed by Universal's Group Accountant before I came. He was unhappy that no one at Lawrensons was taking responsibility for it and many of the forms were wrongly completed."

I begin to see more of what's going on. Chris has more power than I'd appreciated. Universal often exert control through the finance function and, apart from Prior, the Group Accountant is the other Universal man who is frequently in contact with Jim. They've obviously put Chris in to improve our systems and make sure that the accounting function plays its part in providing the controls which Universal are famous for. Considering that this is her brief, she's been remarkably adept at keeping good relationships with all of us though, by the sound of it, she and Marshall are only just speaking to each other.

After Chris has left I ring Jim to see if she can speak at this week's management meeting. He seems a bit doubtful but agrees after I point out that Mike Marshall is at every meeting. I suggest that her presence would be more useful than his on a regular basis.

"Possibly, Phil, but Marshall's been coming for some time and we can't stop him now. And I don't want too many accountants around. They dominate us too much in Universal already. I'm happy for her to come for that agenda item only. We'll discuss the budget first at 8 o'clock on Thursday."

I ring Chris to tell her this and she seems pleased. She asks if an overhead projector can be there and I tell her to fix it with Jim's secretary. I hope she won't go over the top and make too formal a presentation. She may not realize how informal our meetings usually are.

I needn't have worried. She's there at 8 o'clock when I arrive. She's looking composed and confident, sitting at the end of the table next to Jim. He's chatting with her and I can tell that he's coming to like her and to see her value too. Despite what Jim said earlier, I'm sure it won't be long before she's coming to these meetings on a regular basis.

Jim welcomes her and says that we're starting the meeting with a discussion of the budget because Chris and I have concerns about the way we do it. And one of the main reasons for Chris's appointment, he says, was to improve our budgetary control system following comments from Universal's finance function.

Jim knew this, I think to myself. Glancing at Marshall I see the look of resentment in his eyes. He must see Jim's comments as an implied criticism of him. He's bound also to see Chris as an obstacle to his own career progression. There has been talk of someone younger replacing Berisford as Chief Accountant at some point and Marshall must now see her as a potential rival for that job.

Chris stays seated to talk to us and speaks in a clear voice which commands attention. She's a natural speaker, relaxed, just formal enough and very authoritative.

She starts by saying that she came from Universal intending to ensure that the group system operates well but she now sees some problems and conflicts which were not apparent before. And this has made her go back to square one and think what the budgeting system is all about.

"I've drafted out some objectives," she says, "which seem to me to be required from an efficient system. There are three and they are necessary for the three parties involved in the process – Universal top management, the finance function and the operating managers here at Lawrensons. And from what I hear, it's the benefit to you which has been forgotten since Universal took us over."

Everyone's paying close attention, even Wilf who is usually half asleep at meetings unless a technical issue is being discussed. I notice she talks about Universal taking "us" over. I wonder if this is a conscious attempt to identify herself with "us" rather than "them"?

She puts up a slide titled "The Objectives of Budgetary Control". It lists three objectives:

1   TO GIVE UNIVERSAL THE MEANS TO CONTROL LAWRENSONS' OPERATIONS WITHIN AGREED PARAMETERS.

2   TO PROVIDE THE FINANCE FUNCTION WITH CASH AND PROFIT FORECASTS.

3 TO GIVE LAWRENSONS' MANAGERS INFORMA-
TION TO MONITOR, CONTROL AND REVIEW
THEIR PERFORMANCE.

"Is everyone happy with these objectives?"

There's a silence accompanied by a few nods and she carries on. "I've talked to a number of you," she says and I wonder who else she has been talking to. Again I fight to control this ridiculous jealousy. She carries on, "And the atmosphere created by Universal seems to stand in the way of achieving all these objectives. Because all three, in my view, require realistic, achievable figures which everyone is committed to, and that has just not been happening. Am I right?"

The question is posed and accepted as rhetorical. A few more nods and the obvious interest encourages her to go on.

"I have a diagram which shows what ought to happen and what's been happening so far," she says. The matrix she showed me earlier in the week appears again with some extra words in the corners:

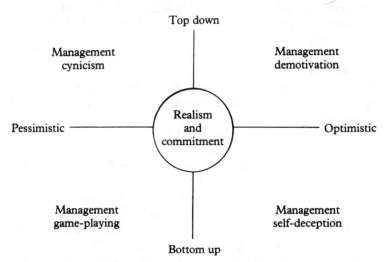

"I'm suggesting that a good budget system achieves all three objectives by having figures in that middle circle which are realistic and to which we are all committed. They're fairly negotiated between what Universal want as a bottom line and what we at Lawrensons can deliver. If we fail to arrive at realistic figures, you have a budget which management don't believe in. They become disillusioned if the top is pressuring them into figures which are not realistic. They start playing games to manipulate the figures and don't really take any notice of later comparisons with actual." Jim takes a deep breath, which is his usual signal that he is going to say something. We all look at him and wonder what his response will be.

"This is all very well," he says. "I accept your model and agree that it's applied here in all four corners since Universal took us over. But I don't see what we can do about it. I try to negotiate realistic figures each time but it isn't always easy. And Universal are under pressure to make a certain return for their shareholders, who aren't always fair and realistic in their demands. What exactly are you suggesting?"

His tone is quite aggressive, at least for Jim who is generally an easy-going sort of chap. But I know from experience that he's very prickly when the relationship with Universal is discussed. He feels under pressure from both sides and doesn't like it.

"I'm suggesting that we do everything we can to negotiate realistic figures with Universal and I accept what you say completely. Mr Prior is under pressure from the Main Board to deliver results for his Division and we're at the end of the chain."

Jim shuffles impatiently in his chair but Chris carries on confidently.

"But I think we should produce a realistic budget for internal purposes anyway. This should be bottom up in the first place with you and the other Directors negotiating to obtain commitments to what you believe to be reasonable levels of performance. I can help with some analysis which will test whether the budget estimates are realistic compared to previous years. For costs which are unrelated to volume or to past performance, there's a technique called zero-base budgeting which goes back to basics and questions the objectives of each department before agreeing spending levels."

Appleby joins in the discussion at this point and I'm slightly surprised to find that he's quite supportive to Chris. She certainly needs some help and I feel that I should have been the one to provide it.

"You've made some very good points, Chris. If you take your argument to its logical conclusion, we end up with two budgets, right?"

She must have been lobbying Appleby too. My jealousy is mixed with admiration at her political skill.

"That's right," she says. "Not that I think it's desirable. The best thing is for our budget and Universal's to harmonize but, if we can't agree realistic figures with Universal, we work internally to our own estimates."

"Producing one budget is bad enough," says Wilf; "it takes no end of effort. Our managers don't have time to produce two and, if we did, we just wouldn't know where we were."

"That's not what worries me," says Jim. "It's how you reconcile the two. I'm responsible to Universal in the end."

It's time I intervened.

"Yes, Jim, I agree, and we as a board must do everything we can to reconcile the two. But we should be asking how best we can motivate our managers to perform well and to exercise control. They don't do this by working to figures which they don't believe in. Maybe we can set the higher levels of achievement as targets that we all strive for if we can. But I think that my chaps are more likely to deliver good performance if we work to achievable budgets which they own and believe in."

Jim sits in silence.

"Where do we go from here?" he asks.

Chris says, "I suggest that we work from a bottom up basis at first without any preconceived constraints. We encourage everyone to be realistic and we stress that there will be some flexibility if the key assumptions change. We have to build up their trust if we are to have realism and commitment."

"And then?", says Jim.

"We assess the figures. I do some analyses to check that the estimates are reasonable compared to previous years and you use your own judgement. I'm sure we'll have to renegotiate in some cases. Then we try to gain acceptance by Universal. But if we can't we still work to our budget and the board manage the gap as best they can."

The discussion goes on a bit longer and Jim, sensing that Appleby and I are in favour of the suggestion, says we can give it a try. Chris explains a bit more about zero-base budgeting and we agree to try it out on a few of the more difficult expense accounts, like personnel, training and office services. Apparently all spending departments have to identify their objectives, the consequences of spending (and of not spending) as well as all other options for providing the resource in a different way. I'm grateful they didn't suggest doing this for some of my sales and marketing costs – it would be a painful exercise for some budgets, like advertising and market research.

Just as I'm preparing to go home later that day, the phone rings and it's Chris.

"I'd just like to thank you for your support this morning, Phil. I was very pleased with the outcome. Your intervention and John's came just at the right time. Do we need to talk further about the budget or can you take it from here?"

"We must keep in touch but I feel reasonably happy at the moment. It's later on that we'll get the problems if the figures aren't good enough for Universal."

"Do you think Jim's committed to having two budget levels if we have to?"

"I don't know. I tried to see him this afternoon but he'd just gone home when I was free."

I clear up my desk and am just going out of the door when the phone rings again. Curiosity drives me to answer it. It's after 6.30 and few people are around at this time.

"Phil?" says an unsteady voice, which at first I don't recognize. "It's Audrey."

Audrey is Jim's wife.

"Phil, can you come to the hospital? Jim's had an accident on the way home and I need someone to be with me. Please." The last few words dissolve into tears.

"How bad is it, Audrey?"

"He's in intensive care. They won't say anything except that he's on the danger list. One leg's broken and there may be internal injuries. Please come quickly."

I run out of the building my emotions in turmoil. As I get into the car I begin to consider the full implications. How can I think of my own career when Jim's life may be hanging on a thread? But I do. And I wonder who's going to take over as acting MD?

Chapter 11

It's nearly two weeks since the accident. I'm sitting at Jim's desk. At last I'm in this seat of power with the big office all to myself, using the expensive mahogany furniture which Jim's father purchased so many years ago. Despite the circumstances which have put me in the MD's chair, I can't help feeling good about the power I feel around me.

I mustn't get carried away. I'm only the acting MD. Jim looks sure to pull through now, though it's been touch and go. And, despite my pleasure at taking over, I've always wanted him to make it. The bond between us over the years has been too strong for me to feel any other way.

Still, the last two weeks have been very interesting. Jim was on the danger list for five days and Audrey stayed at the hospital most of the time. Their two daughters arrived the day after the accident and took over the transport and other arrangements. I was in the office at 8 the following morning and called a management meeting. I had normally chaired our meetings when Jim was away so no one was surprised at this.

It was agreed that I should contact Prior at Universal as soon as he was in his office, usually about 9.30. Appleby suggested that Prior might want to bring forward the new Deputy MD's starting date though Wilf pointed out that it was hardly the best way to introduce a new man. As I left the meeting I began to realize that Prior had little choice but to let me take over for the time being. This filled me with excitement, despite Jim's predicament. Now I felt I had a chance to prove that I can do the top job.

I rang Prior and told him what had happened. There was a long silence and he said he'd ring me back later in the morning. Time dragged until I got the call and the result was what I'd hoped. He wanted me to take over until Jim is fit again.

I mentioned Martyn Ames and whether his move would be brought forward but apparently he can't come for at least two months because of some currency negotiations with the Hong Kong Government. I wondered what would have happened if Ames had been able to come now. Prior said that he'd be available when I needed help and promised to come to see me at least once a week – in normal circumstances he visits monthly.

Much to my surprise, Prior has been very helpful, far more than I expected. On a one-to-one basis he's quite a fair bloke – it's when others are there that he appears rigid and aloof.

The job so far has been unexpectedly easy and without pressure. I'm still handling a few of my sales and marketing duties, though I have delegated most to my Field Sales Manager – Malcolm Davies. Jim's in-tray was nearly empty and little seems to come in the mail each day. What there is I've been able to pass down the line, scribbling Jim's famous phrase – "please deal".

I'm just coming to the stage where I'm wondering what to do. What does a Managing Director do when his in-tray's empty and his action list exhausted?

Remembering that the latest vogue is "management by walking about" I decide to have a wander around the site. I start by going to see Malcolm, who is now established in my office. He's got someone with him – Chris. I haven't seen much of her recently. Indeed I haven't thought of her so much since the accident. Perhaps it was a passing infatuation. But when she flashes her familiar smile my way I know that even my preoccupation with taking over Jim's job is not going to change my underlying feelings.

"Sorry to interrupt," I say.

"That's OK, Phil," she says, "I'm just off. I'll let you

have a costing later on today, Malc."

I find it hard not to resent her being familiar with anyone else but I make sure I don't show it.

"I'll be down to see you a bit later, Chris," I say. "I'd like to see how the budget figures are coming in."

"Fine," she says, "I've got this costing to do, then I'll be free. The budget forms are coming in well and they seem to have taken notice of your memo. They're trying hard to be realistic."

As soon as I established myself in Jim's office, I wrote to all managers with sales or cost responsibility confirming the budget assumptions, reminding them of the budget objectives and stressing the need for sensible, honest figures. All the feedback so far is showing that they are doing just that – all I have to do is to persuade Prior to accept them. Otherwise it will all be in vain.

"I'm glad you've come in, Phil," says Malcolm. "I've had a request for a big contract for own-label pork pies from Kwikmart."

Malcolm handles the Kwikmart account personally as they are our second largest customer.

"You know how I feel about own-label, Malcolm. We lose out on branded sales and we end up losing margin. They all try to screw you down on price once you get into own-label."

"Anyway I've asked Chris to do a costing – she seems more marketing-oriented than Marshall. He just humps costs onto everything."

"It's not just a question of cost, Malc. It's a strategic issue. Jim and his Dad before him always resisted own-brand products. Lose your brand identity and you just become a production unit for the top five retailers."

"I know, Phil, and I agree in principle. But it's happening anyway. Own-label is spreading to almost every outlet. We can't stop it on our own, we're not that powerful. If we turn Kwikmart down, there'll be plenty of others who'll take it. They have spare capacity like us."

I leave Malcolm and walk down to the Production Department. This decision is going to be difficult and there's no one to pass the buck to. That's what being MD means. There may not be too much pressure of work at the moment but now there's pressure of responsibility. I might consult Prior but he wouldn't expect me to ask him for a decision. It's a Lawrensons, not a Universal, matter.

I walk to the pie section and see Appleby on the other side of the production area. Several machines are not being used and, compared to the bread and cakes sections, this department gives an impression of being under-utilized. Managers seem to have more time, operatives are not under pressure and the freezers aren't bursting at the seams as they were a few years ago. Pie sales have come down by over 30 per cent in the last five years and at some time we'll have to consider whether we should pull out altogether.

I walk to meet Appleby and ask if I can have a word. We go into his office. We seem to be getting on better since I took over, which is, I suppose, to be expected. Appleby has good political skills and wants to rise in Universal. I could now be important to his career.

It feels good to think that he can no longer treat me with the slight disdain which was always there when we were peers and, to some extent, competitors. And, to my surprise, I've begun to like him a little and to respect the ability which shines through everything he does.

"Have you heard about the Kwikmart quotation?" he asks me. I'm surprised that he knows already. Malcolm has only just told me.

"Yes, Malcolm's just mentioned it. What do you think?"

"I'm not sure. I was just talking to Chris about it. I've given her some data about our costs if we take it on. She seems to approach this sort of proposal differently from the way Mike Marshall usually does the costings. I'll be interested to see what she comes up with. But I can't afford to lose on the deal. We're already losing money on pies and the margins are the worst of all the product groups."

I carry on with my tour of the site. It makes a big difference, being MD. Everyone notices you and moves around with a new sense of urgency when they see you. They all look up, expecting you to take the lead in a conversation. It's good for my ego and I realize how much I need this power. It will be very hard when the time comes for me to lose it. I walk down to Accounts Department and make for Chris's office. She's working by the side of her computer, adding some figures on a desktop calculator. She looks up and smiles. Her attitude to me hasn't changed. She's still got that confident air and she's still quite casual and informal in conversation. One or two managers have stopped calling me by my first name and either use "Mr Moorley" or leave out my name altogether. But not Chris, and I respect her for it.

"I've got this Kwikmart costing to do, Phil, so I'm not really ready to talk about the budget. Can we meet later?"

"It's about Kwikmart I want to see you actually. Have you done the figures?"

"No, it'll be about an hour. Shall I come to see you then?"

"Yes, that'll be fine."

"I'd also like to talk to you about the management information you're getting as MD. I've been hoping that you'd ask me to help. Your position as MD gives us lots of extra opportunities to get things done. I think the MI going to the chief executive is probably the most important responsibility of the management accountant."

"Fine, Chris, I'd like that, but one thing at a time. Let's look at this Kwikmart decision and get the budget out of the way. Then we can look at my "MI" as you call it. You accountants have all this jargon and initials just to confuse us all."

"MI is shorter than management information," she responds, "but I know what you mean. I'll be in your office at 11.30 with my costing. I'd better talk to you about cost structure and the principles of marginal costing before we look at the actual figures."

"I think I know those principles, Chris, and I'm not sure I want to know more. We've always stood out against marginal pricing for any of our products and I don't want to be the one to start us down that slippery slope."

"I didn't say anything about pricing, Phil. That's your area, not mine. There's an important difference between marginal costing and marginal pricing. But let's wait until I have all the data."

"Shall I involve John and Malcolm too?"

"Why don't you ask them to come in about noon?" she replies, "then we can have half an hour to go through the principles before they come."

I go back to my new office, past Sylvia, Jim's long-serving secretary. She was distraught about his accident but has been much better since he began to improve. She's also largely concealed her well-known disapproval of my broken marriage and subsequent behaviour. Like all the others, she is aware that my approval could now be important to her. I may not quite get the personal cosseting that Jim has been used to but I certainly can't complain about her helpfulness and efficiency. I tell her about my 11.30 meeting with Chris and ask her to request Malcolm and John to come in at midday. She tells me that Prior's rung to say he'll be coming later this afternoon.

I sit at my desk and think about Kwikmart and all the other big retailers who are relentlessly reducing our profitability and killing our brand names. The Kwikmart label is now accepted by the housewife as being good value and their own-label products usually sell at a significant discount to ours. Bread and cakes have hardly suffered so far but it's a matter of time, according to most retail experts. And already over 30 per cent of the pie market is own-brand. Somehow we have to stop the trend if Lawrensons and the other food manufacturers are to retain their identity and profitability.

But we do need the volume to fill our spare capacity. It would be useful to have that extra bit of profit for this year and it will also help us to achieve the ROC which Prior wants in the budget. But all my instincts are against it. We mustn't aim for maximum volume at all costs.

Chris comes at 11.30. It's the first time she's been to see me since I've been in Jim's office. Maybe it's a good thing I've been preoccupied with my new responsibilities. It's stopped me behaving like a lovesick adolescent and shows her that I'm not chasing her or finding excuses to be with her. I can't help feeling proud as I sit opposite her across the polished mahogany table. But I mustn't get too used to this feeling of power because the odds are still against my getting Jim's job on a permanent basis. I must ask Prior about my position with regard to Ames, particularly if, as now looks likely, it will be six months before Jim's back in the saddle.

Chris looks excited and stimulated. Her attitude is so different compared to Marshall's and Berisford's. She is approaching the Kwikmart contract in a positive way, thinking about how we can do it, not looking for reasons why we can't.

She begins by defining marginal cost. "It's the extra money spent as a result of the particular decision you're contemplating. Marginal costing ignores what's already there and looks incrementally at the changes to total cost which will take place."

"That's what worries me, Chris. You can't ignore existing costs in the long term. Someone has to pay them in the end and you can't price everything on a marginal basis."

"You keep going back to price, Phil", she replies, looking slightly pained. "I'm suggesting that marginal costs help you to look at the price options and then make the decision according to your judgement."

She moves to the whiteboard on the office wall and takes a pen in her hand. The familiar instructional style reminds me of the Wednesday evenings when she helped me to understand the financial side of the business. Now I'm MD, I might be able to persuade her to start them again.

"You remember when we first talked about cost structure, I drew you two graphs which showed fixed and variable costs? The variable costs as a slope which increases with volume and fixed costs as a straight line which, from time to time, increases in steps? Well, I'm going to put them together on one graph." She draws on the board:

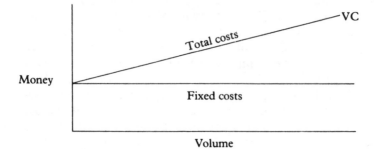

"Now, I'm putting them on one graph to show the *total* cost position, variable on top of fixed. This shows how costs behave until the step in fixed costs takes place."

"Then both fixed and total cost lines will go up," I say, and she nods.

"Now," she continues, "I'm going to add the sales line which converts the graph into a breakeven chart. Can you see how sales will look on the graph?"

"As a diagonal line which moves up with volume, like variable costs, I suppose."

"That's right. You put it in, Phil." She gives me the pen and I draw in:

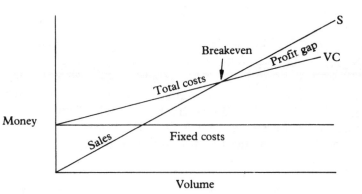

"Right. Now can you see what the gap represents – that gap after total sales cross total costs?"

"Profit," I say, "and the place where the sales and total cost lines cross each other is the breakeven point, isn't it?"

"That's right and you can read it off either axis of the graph, in terms of money or volume."

"I understand this, Chris, but I'm not sure of its relevance to the Kwikmart deal. That will never break even at the prices they want for own-label."

"It is of relevance because Lawrensons as a whole has a cost structure like this and is over breakeven. We're into that profit gap and we have a chance to take more business which, as long as it covers the extra costs, will give us extra contribution to improve our profit."

We're both standing at the board and she draws into the profit gap another line:

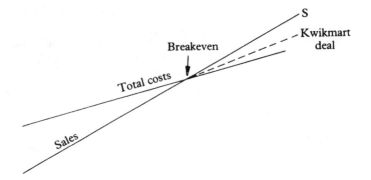

"You see, Phil, the Kwikmart deal is at a lower price level than our mainstream business, thus the sales line slopes more gently. But it still covers the variable costs. What we have to be careful about is any step increase in fixed costs which must be taken into the evaluation. The sales from this deal must cover this step as well as the variable costs."

She draws a further line within the profit gap:

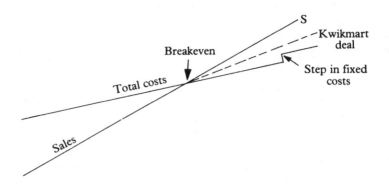

"As long as the contribution over the variable costs covers that step, we're OK, at least on financial grounds. Shall we have a look at the figures from Kwikmart? I've got the information on costs from John. In fact the margins are quite low – well under 10 per cent – though that's after including the extra step in fixed costs."

She writes up these figures:

Sales per month	274,000
Variable production costs	(234,000)
Extra step in fixed costs	(15,000)
Contribution	25,000

"OK, so Malcolm's sales forecast is £274,000. The normal variable costs of material, labour, energy, distribution, etc. are £234,000 and the £15,000 is the extra we spend on costs which are normally fixed but which have to be increased specifically as a result of this project."

"Like what?"

"Re-tooling machines, an extra supervisor for the evening shift, another man in the quality control team and one or two other odds and sods."

"Are you saying that we should take this contract, even at such a low margin?"

"I'm not the decision maker. You and Malcolm are, I'm just presenting the financial reality. This contract will increase our bottom line by £300,000 per annum – you must decide whether you can afford to turn it down."

"How can I when you put it like that?"

"By comparing it with the money we can make by using the capacity in other ways. Also by weighing the short-term profit advantages against the long-term strategic issues. Shall we prepare some questions for Malcolm and John when they come?"

"All right then, you suggest some."

"You too. You know the business better than I do. Let me start off."

She writes up:

HOW ELSE MIGHT WE USE THE CAPACITY TAKEN BY THE CONTRACT?

"It's not just right now," I say. "What other ways might we use it in the future?"

"Right," she replies, "often some other deal comes up just when you've committed yourselves to one with lower profit. So another key question is:"

HOW LONG ARE WE COMMITTED TO THE KWIKMART CONTRACT?

"I expect they'll want a year's guarantee at least," I say.

"Then we might have a problem, Phil. Marginally priced contracts should always be short-term commitments if at all possible."

"That's exactly my point. This is a strategic move and we shouldn't just choose short-term contribution without thinking about the long term."

I'm beginning to warm to this idea of listing questions and add a few of my own. "There's a couple more things I'd like to ask Appleby, Chris."

"Why don't you call him John?" she asks. "You call everyone else by their Christian names."

I ignore this comment and give her a critical look. Now I'm acting MD, I can call people what I like. It's no bad thing for Chris to be reminded that her confident air can go too far and I notice with pleasure that she sees this. She goes red and some beads of sweat come down her forehead. She can be ruffled after all, I think to myself, and somehow it warms me towards her even more. I carry on:

"Let's ask Appleby what effect an own-label contract will have on his existing output."

"In terms of cost, you mean? I've worked that out."

"No, just general effect. Quality and flexibility. I'm thinking particularly of his supervisors. They'll be distracted away from our branded products."

She writes up:

WHAT WILL BE THE EFFECTS ON PRESENT PRODUCTION OPERATIONS?

"OK," she says, "anything else?"

"Yes," I reply, "I'd like to be sure there aren't any other extra costs which you've not taken into account."

"We went through them pretty thoroughly."

"Yes, but have you only included production? What about administration? Extra wages clerks for the extra staff. Extra work for your department. And what about the cost of our time?"

"That's not a marginal cost, Phil. Our salaries are paid anyway and the effect on management time and effort has to be part of your final judgement. But I agree that we should check on other costs. There's also sales administration for instance, though order processing and invoicing on own-label is fairly straight-forward."

ARE THERE ANY OTHER EXTRA FIXED COSTS WHICH HAVE NOT BEEN TAKEN INTO ACCOUNT?

"And there's the last question, the key one," she says. I look at her quizzically because I can't think of any more.

"The effect on existing price structure and volume," she continues.

"That goes without saying," I reply, "and that's why I'm going to turn it down."

"Hang on a minute, Phil. The decision should take into account the contribution from existing sales which we shall lose if we take on this contract. But we shouldn't take contribution which would be lost anyway. So the real question is – what will happen if we don't get the contract? If someone else does it, we lose the volume, and the prices are pushed down anyway. So we'd be mad not to take the contribution we can get from doing it ourselves."

"I wish I knew what the competitors would do," I say.

"Could you find out?"

"Possibly. Jim used to be in touch with the MDs of the big four. I'll think about it. But I'm reasonably sure what the answer will be. We're all desperate for volume."

She nods as if she'd guessed it all along and writes up:

WHAT CONTRIBUTION WILL WE LOSE FROM EXIST-ING PRODUCTS? (WHICH WE WON'T LOSE ANYWAY)

"Right, Phil," she says, "I think we're all set. If you're

happy that John and Malcolm can satisfy you on all these questions, you should take the contract. At least on financial grounds."

"What do you mean – on financial grounds?"

"Well, I'm only the management accountant, your financial advisor. You've got to weigh the answers to all these questions against your long-term view, your gut feeling if you like. But you've got to be sure that your reservations justify turning down £300,000 per annum at the bottom line."

"But I still don't like that low margin. It's under 10 per cent and that gives very little scope for error."

"Which reminds me of another question, Phil."

She writes up:

ARE OUR MARGINS PROTECTED IF COSTS GO UP FROM PRESENT ESTIMATES?

"We must have cost change provisions," she says, "otherwise we face the classic fixed-price contract problem. Most of the own-label contracts I've seen have some inflation factor built in. But your general point is valid. We must keep costs down. We can't afford to let any inefficiency creep in. Though there is one reason why we are justified in accepting lower margins."

"What's that?"

"The lower level of sales and marketing resource. Nearly 10 per cent of our fixed costs are selling and marketing, most of which don't apply to own-brand. So that margin is not a million miles away from what we normally get from pies if you exclude sales and marketing costs."

I could kick myself for not seeing this obvious point before. It could make all the difference. How useful it is to have someone to talk through these issues. And someone who thinks commercially too.

"You really do think like a businessman, sorry woman, Chris. You don't sound like an accountant at all."

"Good management accountants should be commercial. And I want to be a good one. I need to see the business just as broadly as you."

"You're doing well," I say, rather embarrassed by my compliment to her. I've never found it easy to praise though I know I should do it more, particularly now I'm in the top job. She seems pleased and we both smile, our eyes meeting for a shade too long. Just at that moment Sylvia comes in.

"Mr Appleby and Mr Davies are here. Shall I show them in?"

The four of us have an hour's intensive discussion. The others seem surprised by the questions on the board and it seems as if I'm putting them through the third degree. But I get all the answers I want.

Appleby's fairly sure that accepting the own-label deal is not going to restrict us from taking on other business. If existing markets improve or other contracts come up, we can increase the evening shift. Malcolm reckons that we can restrict our commitment to a year with an interim six-month price review and, if necessary, we can pull out by putting up the price at that point.

Appleby is convinced that he can absorb the production without adversely affecting existing operations and that Chris has taken all the expected production cost increases into account. The main unknown on cost is the meat price, and we agree that the contract must contain a clause to vary price with raw material cost changes. Appleby says he will hold all the other costs. I notice how his attitude has, like mine, changed since this morning and he's now working on the premise that we should accept the contract but first examine the potential problems. I think Chris has rather subtly achieved this by her way of posing the issue. It gives us £25,000 a month on the bottom line – we would have to have some good reasons for turning it down.

The penultimate question clinches it. What contribution will we lose from existing business? Malcolm firmly believes that we shall lose out on existing sales anyway so we are not protecting margin or volume by holding out on our own. No other pie supplier is going to say no to Kwikmart in the present climate. Malcolm even takes the view that being involved in own-label supplies will help us put our brands in the stores and cut down on the distribution costs.

Rather than deciding immediately, I say that I'll think

about it and maybe ring the MD of our biggest competitor. I don't admit it to them but I also think I'll have a word with Prior this afternoon. And, at Chris's suggestion, Malcolm agrees to talk to Kwikmart again to see if there's a chance of getting a better margin. She makes the point that the price should not be marginal unless it's the maximum we can get while still keeping the business.

As they all get up to leave the office, I ask Chris to stay.

"What are you doing for lunch?" I ask.

"I'm working through. I have done every day since the budget forms started coming in."

"Can we talk about the budget over lunch? I'll ask Sylvia to fetch some sandwiches."

"How can I say no to the boss?" she replies with a smile.

She tells me that all the managers seem to be playing the budget game fairly. One or two were putting extra fat into their cost estimates but she pointed out that the increases were excessive compared to past years and they agreed to bring them down.

"Any idea what the bottom line's going to look like?"

"I'm not certain but it looks even better than when we did our early estimate a few weeks ago. I think that a 10 per cent return is quite possible and, if we clinch the Kwikmart deal, it will help a lot. Can you see how it will help return on capital, Phil?"

"Yes, profit will increase while capital employed will remain the same so the return will increase. Right?"

"Right."

Yet something stirs at the back of my mind.

"Chris," I say, "what about working capital? Won't stock and debtors increase?"

She looks ruffled for the second time today. "I think those evening lessons are paying off. That's exactly the sort of question I should have asked myself."

"And that a managing director should ask his management accountant?"

"Very much so. You should have enough knowledge and confidence to keep me on the ball. I'll have to ask John about increases in stock levels and Malcolm about payment terms. We must keep the working capital down if we are to reap the full benefit. And, if it's significant, I should include some interest charges on the working capital in my costing."

"Anyway, going back to the budget, when will you have a first draft for me?"

"On Monday, all being well. Shall we fix a meeting?"

"Yes, and I'm going to sound out Prior this afternoon. I'll try to gauge what he's looking for."

Sylvia brings the sandwiches with some coffee on a silver tray. We start to chat generally. Chris asks me how I'm getting on in the new role.

"I'm enjoying it at the moment, almost too much. I know it can't last."

"It might. I hear Jim's going to be six months at least. And, with only three years or so to his retirement, do you think they'll ask him to come back?"

"Possibly not. But there's your Mr Ames poised to join us in two months. He must still be the favourite."

"I guess so," says Chris, "but they'll be in a difficult position if you do very well. I reckon you will and I think I can help you."

"You've helped a lot already. Like this morning, for instance. That meeting about Kwikmart was one of the best I've had for a long time. It reminded me of the old days. Your influence is good for all of us."

"Can I look at your management information then?"

"Yes. But, as I said, when we've put the budget to bed."

Though we've finished our business, we chat on until the lunch hour is over. Chris asks me questions about Jean and the kids. I tell her about Angela's passion for horses and she tells me she loved to ride when she was in her teens. She says she'd like to meet my children and I say I'd like that too. We agree to fix lunch together one weekend when I have the two of them for a day. I wonder what the kids will think and how I'll react to seeing her away from work? It can only make my feelings stronger but there's no way in the world that I'm going to miss the chance.

Prior arrives at about 4 pm. He listens to the Kwikmart story. He tends to listen with an expression of intense concentration on his face which can be very inhibiting. He seems to be weighing up and questioning every phrase in his mind. He's a typical Universal senior manager. A lot of presence, a sharp mind and a fixation on the bottom line. After I've finished he says:

"I don't think you need me to tell you what to do, Phil. It sounds as if you've made up your mind anyway. If we could stop own-label we would, but it's a fact of life. If it's going to happen anyway, we might as well make what we can from it."

His point finally convinces me. No need to ring up the competition. They'll all think like Prior. And, if I can get the deal signed up quickly, I can stop the competition being given a chance to earn the contribution themselves.

Next we discuss the budget. I explain the problems of previous years and how the Universal influence affects the way the budget is used for control purposes. As he looks me in the eye with that appraising expression, I wonder if I should have been so frank. He takes a deep breath and walks to the window.

"Jim's never mentioned this, Phil, but I've had the same comments from some of our other MDs. You must remember that we have goals which we must achieve for our shareholders. The most important thing is that we negotiate to achieve your objectives and mine."

I can hardly believe my ears. Just what I'd hoped he would say.

"You presumably must have some idea what profit levels you're looking for next year?" I say speculatively,.

"Well, your profits have been lousy for the last three years. Oh, I know that the food industry's generally got problems, but the other parts of the Group can't go on funding you for ever. What's your ROC going to be this year?"

Two months ago I would have stood open-mouthed. Now I can say: "We'll make about 2 million on assets of 36 million. Not even 6 per cent, I'm afraid."

"Yes, and that's before tax. I'm not making any firm demands at this stage – I'll need to look at your figures. But we must move into double figures at the very least."

I remember Chris's comment earlier today and think that at least it's within reach. I tell Prior that I'll contact him next week to discuss the first draft informally.

"Yes, Phil. That's a good idea. Then at least we'll know where we stand before it's too formal. I'm glad you're approaching it this way, it means we can work together."

I'm pleased to hear this. Compliments don't come easily from people like Prior and I feel that I'm building bridges for the future.

I ask about Ames and my position when he comes.

"You'll still be acting MD and Martyn will work for you in the first instance. But I can't make any promises for the future, you know that. And Jim will be back fairly soon after Martyn joins us, or at least we hope so."

As I go back to my flat that evening, I feel elated. Things are going well. I'm hitting it off with Prior, Ames is going to work for me in the first instance and we're very close to having a budget which we're all committed to. As I pour myself a gin and tonic, the doorbell rings. It's Jean.

She's never visited me at the flat before and she looks terribly drawn. I ask her to come in, and pour her a drink. She also likes a gin and tonic when she needs calming down.

"It's Angela, Phil. She's been playing truant from school. The Head Teacher wants to see us both the day after tomorrow. Please can you come?"

Just when things were looking good. Angela was always the stable, good-natured one. How can this have happened? As Jean sits back on my settee, drink in hand, she manages a tired smile.

She still looks amazingly attractive and I remember why I married her.

Chapter 12

I'm sitting in the Headmistress's office with Jean by my side. It's two days after she came to see me. We spent yesterday evening with Angela, trying to find out what's behind the sudden change in behaviour. She was sullen and uncooperative – totally unlike anything I had seen before. We just couldn't get through to her and gave up after about an hour.

Afterwards Jean and I discussed how it had happened and what we should do. Apparently it had been as big a shock to Jean as it was to me. Until the Headmistress rang, she had no idea what had been going on but, as soon as Angela was confronted, all communication between them stopped.

Despite all the bitterness of the last few years, Jean has been marvellous about this and one good thing that has come out of it is the chance that we can have a civilized relationship again, perhaps even take the children out together some weekends. She could easily have blamed me for Angela's behaviour but she hasn't. She talked rationally about our split but avoided any question of blame. This crisis might help us both to think constructively about our future.

The Headmistress is talking to us rather patronizingly about the problems of children from broken homes.

"And twelve to thirteen is such a difficult age anyway. They begin to develop physically when they aren't really emotionally able to cope with it."

She obviously fancies herself as an amateur psychologist

and I want to argue but steel myself to keep quiet.

"The district psychologist tells me that Angela's behaviour is very common in such circumstances. We must work together to help her to come through it."

The Headmistress asks us to come again in two weeks' time after the psychologist's report and promises to let us know immediately if Angela fails to turn up for school. I go back to their house (it seems strange to call it "theirs" but that's what it is, even though I still pay the mortgage) and we have another talk to Angela. We ask Mark – her younger brother, always so close to her despite the three-year gap – if he knows what's wrong, but he seems as perplexed as we are. Before I go, Angela seems to be coming round a bit but, just as I'm putting on my coat, she rushes upstairs crying hysterically. Jean tells me to go and I know she's right. We say goodbye and I wonder whether to kiss her cheek, just as I might with a friend. But I don't.

Next morning I find it difficult to concentrate on work. For the first time in ages, I'm seeing my family as an important part of my life. And despite the circumstances, I quite like the feeling.

Sylvia comes in with a telex.

"It's from Hong Kong, Mr Moorley," she says. "Mr Ames is flying over on Saturday and will be in to see you on Monday morning with Mr Prior."

This brings me down to earth with a bump. My power as acting MD at Lawrensons is only temporary and soon I'll have to cope with a deputy who'll be trying to beat me to the top job. Relations will be difficult to say the least.

Chris phones. "I've got the first draft budget out, Phil. Can I bring it in?"

"Of course," I say. "It had better be good."

Sitting in my office five minutes later, she politely takes me to task for that comment. "You really shouldn't say things like 'it'd better be good', Phil. It won't affect me but comments like that can put pressure on an accountant to produce the figures you want, not those which are objective and correct."

I take her point. Management accountants should produce the information managers need to make decisions, not what they want to see to keep them happy. Their role is becoming clearer in my mind all the time.

"All right then, let's see the figures," I say.

She walks over to my whiteboard. She writes up:

	This year	Preliminary budget	Latest budget
Sales	106,250	113,541	117,901
Variable costs	73,140	78,372	81,406
Contribution	33,110	35,169	36,495
Production costs	8,500	8,500	8,429
Profit before fixed ind.	24,610	26,669	28,066
Fixed indirects	22,620	23,687	24,203
Profit	1,990	2,982	3,863
Fixed assets	16,828	19,829	19,829
Current assets	30,411	37,203	32,482
Total assets	47,239	57,032	52,311
Current liabilities	11,161	11,928	12,040
Net assets	36,078	45,104	40,271
Return on capital	5.5%	6.6%	9.6%

"Not quite the 10 per cent we wanted," I say, "but good compared to last year and to the other figures. What do you mean by preliminary budget?"

"Those are the estimates we worked out in our evening sessions. They were only approximate figures. I've now worked it through much more carefully."

"What are the main differences?"

"We're up on sales by about £4.5 million. That's the Kwikmart contract and the more exact effect of the price increase from 1 April, worked through product by product. I think it's because we sell more in the last half of the year when we'll benefit from the higher prices."

"We're up a bit on costs, aren't we?"

"Yes. For variable costs it's the effect of the Kwikmart contract. Also, materials and labour turned out to be slightly higher than we thought. For fixed costs, there are higher budgets in one or two areas. Research and marketing mainly."

"But what about the assets? They're well down."

"Yes. It's debtors. I had a word with Malcolm and he thinks he can achieve the sales budget without increasing debtors. That's why the current assets are so much down. He told me you'd spoken to him about that."

When I handed my duties over to Malcolm after Jim's accident, I made it an urgent priority for him to look at the debtors position. I reminded him of the cash flow implications and of the effect on return on capital. The combination of surprise and puzzlement on his face made me think that maybe he needs some finance lessons too. But he's taken action so our budgeted profitability is looking better.

"We need to trim costs to bring profits up to 10 per cent, don't we?" I say. "About £400,000. Can we have another look at those marketing and research budgets?"

"I already have and they seem fair and reasonable to me. It's the easy way – cutting back on those sort of costs, but you suffer in the long term. I've had a look at the admin. and personnel budgets and, after using the zero-base approach, I reckon a saving of £100,000 or so is possible without too much problem. Otherwise I think it's all more or less realistic. Why not put these figures up to Universal as they stand?"

I agree to have a word with Prior when he comes on Monday. It's better to see him in person rather than talk over the phone. But I'll try to have Ames out of the way while we're discussing it. Don't want him intervening if I can help it. Chris agrees to refine the cost figures after further discussion with administration and personnel and then produce a final draft for me to see Prior. I expect her to go but she stays on.

"Is there anything else you want, Chris?" I say.

"Yes. You said we could discuss your management information needs once we've dealt with the budget."

"You're very persistent, aren't you? And we haven't really

finished the budget yet, have we? But all right. Tell me what you want."

"It's more what you want, Phil. From my short while here I can see that management information needs have never really been thought through in any organized way. You get far too much paper with far too much data and I bet you hardly ever look at it."

I think about the monthly reporting pack which shows budget against actual for all the departments and the overall company results. Pages and pages of figures. They're always passed at management meetings with hardly any comment and I think I know why. No one ever looks at them, including Jim, I suspect. He once told me how it had all become much more complex since the Universal takeover, so all he looks at is the bottom line. The bottom line, that phrase again. I tell Chris about this.

"OK," she says, "I reckon that's partly why you've had a mental block about finance. There's too much paper with too many figures on."

"Before Universal, the old man used to insist on one sheet of paper with all the key data on it."

"That's exactly how I want to approach it. It sounds as if old Mr Lawrence was ahead of his time. But I wonder if he really picked out the important things on his one bit of paper. One of the principles of management information is that you focus on the key success variables, the things which are really important to doing well in your job. Can you do that?"

"For which job? As MD?"

"Yes. As far as you can. What do you need to know about to run this business well? I'll write them up and we'll also think about how frequently you need the information. And forget about what you get now, what Universal want or what we can produce. Think about *your* needs. And don't forget, you're a general manager now, not just a marketing man."

I take her point and begin to think.

People are my most important responsibility as MD. The staff and their level of morale. Does she intend that I include this aspect? I ask her.

"Of course," she says, "you're getting the idea. How do you assess staff morale?"

"By walking around and seeing them, I suppose."

"Yes, but we can't include that in a management information report. There are quantitative indicators, aren't there? Every personnel specialist will tell you."

I look puzzled and she explains. "Labour turnover and absentee records. You should be seeing graphs of these trends at least once a month."

"Graphs? We never have graphs."

"And why not? Because no one's thought about your needs. If you're like every other sales and marketing man, you prefer them to numbers, don't you? And in this case it's the trend in turnover and sickness which is important, not the absolute figures."

"Isn't it George Dixon's job to do this?"

"Possibly. But usually in organizations people don't think of their responsibilities for producing information to others. It needs someone to bring it all together and that's what I'm trying to do. In any case the information comes from Wages Section, which is a Finance Department. Now, what else?"

"Sales volume, I suppose."

"Just volume, or income too?"

"Both, I suppose."

"And average price per ton?"

"Yes."

"By product group or in total?"

"By product group."

"How often?"

We go on like this for two hours, covering production, sales, admin. – the lot – until my brain hurts. I'm relieved when Sylvia comes in to tell me that George Dixon's here for a meeting about the proposed subcontracting of the catering facilities.

My whiteboard is full of ideas for information. My mind is full of concepts which Chris has been describing to me. Management by exception – only receive information about things which vary from the normal pattern. Key success variables – focus on those things which are really important.

Decision focus – concentrate on information which helps you to make future decisions, don't just receive information because it's "nice to know". She asks if she can come back later to take notes from the whiteboard.

"How will you put all that lot on one piece of paper, Chris?" I ask and she laughs.

"I'll try," she says. "It might be two. But remember, this will be all you receive. I won't give you the detailed workings as most accountants do. You'll just have the relevant indicator and, if you want more, you ask for it. At your level, you shouldn't have detail unless you can use it for a particular purpose."

As she walks out of my office past George Dixon he glances down at her legs. George used to compete with me for the title of company stud and he greets me with a knowing smile.

"That's some crumpet, Phil. How are you getting on there?"

I give him a look which cuts him dead and ignore his comment. He looks embarrassed.

"I'm sorry, Phil," he stammers.

"Look, forget it, George. She's a nice girl and I'm now acting MD, right?"

He looks at me pensively and I wonder what he's thinking. Perhaps how stuck up I've become since I took over Jim's job. I'd rather he think that than guess the real reason why I'm so protective towards Chris.

After our meeting I ask George to get a costing of the catering department from Mike Marshall to compare with the outside quote. I have a working lunch and the afternoon flies by. The job is so involving and all-embracing. I know that I'll never again be satisfied with a sales and marketing role and I begin to feel that I'm actually cut out for general management.

I remember suddenly that it's Friday and the weekend stretches ahead like an empty void. I haven't arranged to see the kids – it isn't my turn to have them, and we felt it best not to disturb the pattern. So I spend a lonely weekend with little to do but watch some television and fix some shelves in the bedroom.

Monday morning comes as a release. The meeting with

Prior and Ames will get the adrenalin flowing again. I arrive at 7.30 to clear my mail and have a final look at the budget figures. Chris has, as promised, left the final draft for me and the cost reductions have increased profit slightly. The return will be 9.8 per cent. I'm determined that, as a matter of principle, Prior's going to accept this. If I allow him arbitrarily to put it up, I shall lose credibility, the managers will lose motivation and we'll be back to the attitudes of previous years.

Prior and Ames arrive late morning. Sylvia is flushed when she comes to tell me they've arrived. I soon see why. Martyn Ames is the sort of man who makes middle-aged ladies twitter. He's well over six foot, fair hair, bronzed face with a relaxed confident air. His suit is of a superior cut and he wears it with style. I feel far smaller than my 5ft 9in as I walk out to greet him, but I do my best to match his confidence.

Prior asks how Jim is progressing and I give him the latest bulletin. He's now officially off the danger list and non-family visitors will be allowed next week.

"Do they still think about six months?" asks Prior and I nod. Ames looks unconcerned and says nothing.

Prior proceeds to ask about the budget. I try to get rid of Ames by suggesting that he take a trip around the site but he says he'd like to go after lunch. I feel irritated but there's little I can do. Ames is a smooth operator. I'm afraid he won't miss the chance to demonstrate his superior knowledge of finance if he can.

"Have you got some preliminary figures?" Prior asks.

"Yes," I say, "but it's only a draft. We haven't prepared the forms for the full presentation yet."

"Just give us the bottom line, Phil. That's all we need in Universal, isn't that right, Martyn?" He looks at Ames.

"Too right," says Ames, "and the return on capital. Give them 20 per cent and Universal won't complain."

"That may be fine in the detergents market in Hong Kong," I say, trying to keep calm. "The food industry in this country is a different kettle of fish."

"Yes, we know that, Phil," says Prior, "or at least I do. Martyn's been away from the UK for a while. Doesn't know how the supermarkets screw us down on margins."

Round one to me, I think, but Ames looks unperturbed. I produce the final summary which Chris has prepared for me. I deliberately don't give Ames a copy and he has to look over Prior's shoulder.

	This year	Budget
Sales	106,250	117,901
Variable costs	73,140	81,406
Contribution	33,110	36,495
Production costs	8,500	8,429
Profit before fixed ind.	24,610	28,066
Fixed indirects	22,620	24,108
Profit	1,990	3,958
Fixed assets	16,828	19,829
Current assets	30,411	32,482
Total assets	47,239	52,311
Current liabilities	11,161	12,040
Net assets	36,078	40,271
Return on capital	5.5%	9.8%

Prior lets out a soft whistle.

"You've surprised me, Phil. I wanted 10 per cent, but I never thought you'd come near it this year."

"We haven't yet," I reply. "It's only a budget, but it's one that we're committed to and one that we'll deliver."

"Could I just have a look, Paul?" says Ames, using Prior's Christian name confidently. I wish I could pluck up the courage to do so.

"These current assets are far too high, surely," he says. "I'd like to see how they're split between stock and debtors and what the ratios to sales are."

This infuriates me and I have to struggle to avoid hitting him.

"You'll have the chance when you start here, Mr Ames," I say sharply, "but I can assure you that we are very aware of the need to control working capital. The first draft budget showed 72 days debtors and we've brought it down to 57. But getting money out of these multiple chains is bloody difficult. If you've got some ideas once you start, I'll be delighted to delegate the task of collection to you."

I have the feeling that Prior is quite pleased at the way I put Ames down. But I wonder if I should be more careful. If Ames is ever my boss, I'll need his favour and I'm making that somewhat unlikely.

"What do you think?" I ask Prior. "Can we go ahead?"

Prior looks back at me.

"I'd like to see 10 per cent, Phil. But you said you wanted to own the budget. Are you sure that the figures have sufficient stretch in them?"

Thinking about this I'm not all that sure. If I'm expecting Prior to trust me, I must see each manager and check that all the assumptions and performance levels are realistic, achievable and without slack. Chris said she'd been through them but I must also check personally.

"I think so, but I'll have one final check. If I am sure, will you except this as my bottom line commitment?"

"I will, but on one condition. That you accept that even 10 per cent is not an acceptable return in the long term. It's a step in the right direction. But when we next produce our long-term plans, I want to see this budget as the first step towards a return which justifies the risk of Universal's investment."

I accept this point, though I know that I might not be the one who has to deliver the undertaking. Then I put Ames on the spot too.

"What do you think, Mr Ames? You're going to be part of the team."

"Of course," he says, "we have to deliver the bottom line and a return to justify Universal's faith in us. I'm looking forward to working with you to achieve it. And I hope you'll call me Martyn."

His friendly smile makes me wonder if I've misjudged him. Just then Sylvia comes in to tell me that we're ready for lunch. We're just walking out of my office when the phone rings.

"Tell them to ring back," I say. We're just outside the building when Sylvia calls me back.

"Mr Moorley," she says. "It's Jean – Mrs Moorley. It sounds like an emergency."

I excuse myself and walk into my office.

"Phil," says Jean, "the school have just rung. Angela left after morning break and she's not come back. Someone saw her with some lads on motorbikes. I think we should call the police. Please come."

I'm just going to tell her that it's impossible when I begin to think about my life. Maybe my work is the most important thing for me now but I can't shirk my responsibility for the children. And perhaps I'd be better off trying to develop a relationship with Jean again than mooning over a young girl like Chris. I know what I have to do. I tell Prior and Ames that they'll have to lunch on their own.

Chapter 13

Exactly a week later I'm in my office with George Dixon. He's going on at great length about the benefits of subcontracting the catering and I'm hardly listening to him. He's one of those people who will never say one word when ten will do, particularly when it's his own pet subject. And he never takes any hints from those he's boring.

My mind wanders back to the last week. The desperate afternoon driving round looking for Angie. The message from the police that they had found her alone, cold and crying in a street five miles away. The tearful reunion, the long night sitting up talking it out and the dreadful realization that her trauma definitely was caused by the breaking up of our marriage. She even admitted that she had hoped it would bring us back together again.

The weekend was great. The family back together again, spending the Sunday as we used to in the old days – swimming and eating a snack lunch in the leisure centre. But for Jean and me it wasn't quite like the old days. We both sensed that the old spark wasn't there and, on Jean's insistence, I went back to the flat each evening.

A few weeks earlier I might have tried harder. Now I find that I just can't push Chris out of my mind – her youth and enthusiasm put everything else in the shade, even the woman I married all those years ago and whom, until a few weeks ago, I wanted back so desperately.

Prior was very good about my rushing off and missing

lunch with him and Ames. He asked after Angela and assured me that I need not worry. All in all I find him a good man to work for. Martyn Ames also rang the next day and asked how things were, reassuring me that he'd had a useful visit despite my absence. I was just thinking that maybe I'd mis-judged him and that I was merely jealous of his looks and style when he gave me cause to dislike him even more.

"Your management accountant took me through the budget, Phil," he said, and I silently cursed his easy assumption of my Christian name. "She's a remarkable lady. I'm looking forward to working with her."

I felt like reminding Chris that she shouldn't have given him access to the budget information, but I realized that would be silly. But I just can't face anyone else getting close to her, particularly someone so obviously attractive and nearer to her age group. I must find out if he's married.

"And the costing produced by Mike Marshall is well over the quote, so I think we must go ahead. Can I put that recommendation to the management meeting with your bless-ing?"

George Dixon is expecting me to speak. I give him one of my standard replies in such circumstances.

"There are a lot of factors to take into account, George. I'd like to think it over before letting you know my decision. Has Chris Goodhart approved the figures?"

"No, but she's got a copy and she's come back with a few questions so she's fully in the picture."

As George goes out I focus on the paper that he's left in front of me and try to start thinking more carefully about what he's trying to do. All right, perhaps he can save some money, but the effect on morale of sacking existing staff and bringing in subcontractors is likely to be serious. As acting MD I don't want to be associated with such a move unless the reasons are compelling. On the other hand, George's figures claim we can save over £100,000 p.a., so can we ignore such a benefit to profits?

I look at the latest estimate costing for this year:

Wages	172,000
Food costs	208,000
Depreciation on equipment	30,000
Crockery and cutlery	7,000
Manager's salary	16,000
Other expenses	11,500
Central indirect costs	28,500
	473,000

George compared this figure with a quote from a local catering firm of £365,000, giving an exact saving of £108,000.

How can an outside company, who need to cover their own overheads and make a profit undercut us by so much? George said that Chris has a copy, and it would be an excuse to see her. She's so good at helping me to see these financial issues more clearly.

She's in my office in five minutes. That's one of the advantages of being MD – I feel I can ask people to come to my office and they usually come straight away.

She sits at my table, as attractive and enthusiastic as ever. Before I can ask her about the catering, she says how pleased she is that Prior has accepted the budget. I remind her that it's all still subject to my completing the interviews with the managers and to the final presentation to Group.

"I know, but the Group Accountant told me that he'd heard it would be OK from Prior. I think you've done extremely well to get it through and I'm delighted. It means we actually have good figures to control ourselves against. And all the managers are pleased."

The budget has been a triumph for her too – the managers trusted her by producing realistic estimates and her reputation will now grow accordingly. If Prior hadn't accepted their figures, they would have felt let down.

I ask her about the catering costing. "I don't really like subcontracting, Chris, but £100,000 is too much to reject. Have you checked the figures? I understand that Marshall produced them."

"They're OK as a costing, Phil, but they don't reflect the true effect of the decision to subcontract. The real benefits will be far less in practice. I've done a cash flow evaluation for the first three years and it's much closer than it appears."

"Why cash flow? Aren't Marshall's figures cash?"

"No. They're existing costs. They represent the amounts now being spent. But, to evaluate this decision, we need to examine the future impact. We need to look forward, to calculate what we can really save if we subcontract. That's what management accounting means – looking forward."

"I'm still not sure what you're driving at," I say. "You'd better do your usual act on my whiteboard."

She writes across the board – Year 1, Year 2, Year 3, – and then down the page all the cost headings.

"OK," she says, "wages first. We shall save £172,000 for three years, but there are redundancy costs of about £45,000. We must take those into the evaluation."

I nod in agreement though I'm not sure how she's going to do it. She writes up:

	Year 1	Year 2	Year 3	Total
Wages	+ 172	+ 172	+ 172	+ 516
Redundancy	− 45	–	–	− 45

"You see, I'm building up a project cash flow – showing the effect on the bank account of this decision. We save 172 but we pay out 45 if we close the department."

"All right," I say, "so the plus means it's a cost we have now, a minus means it's a cost of closing."

"In a way, yes, but that's not the best way to see it. Forget what's happening now, just think about the future cash flow effect of closure. We save £172 per annum by closing."

"Isn't that the same thing?"

"Not necessarily. For instance, one of the costs is depreciation. Do I include that in my cash flow?"

After a moment's thought I see what she means. Depreciation is a running cost of the department but you can't save it. It's a book entry reflecting past investment.

"All right, Chris. I take your point. But what do we put

in for equipment? That has a book value, doesn't it?"

"Yes. I've got it here," she says, looking into her file. "We bought it for £240,000 and it's being depreciated over 8 years. It's now on the books at £90,000 because we've had it five years."

"What shall we sell it for?"

"Well, it's part of the deal that the caterers take it over. George negotiated a price of £40,000."

"What! That's a loss of £50,000. That will go against this year's profits, won't it?"

"Yes, but it's not a cash flow. It's just a book entry, telling the shareholders about the loss that's been made. In the cash flow we just show the £40,000 cash."

"But what about the depreciation that's no longer charged in the profit and loss account?"

"We ignore that too," she replies. "You see, they're self-cancelling. You could include them on both sides but the difference will be £40,000 anyway."

In response to my pained expression, she writes some figures on the other side of the board.

Bought five years ago		240,000		
Depreciation	30,000			
	30,000			
	30,000			
	30,000			
	30,000	150,000		
Book value		90,000		
	Sell			Keep
Sale price	40,000	Depreciation	30,000	
			30,000	
Loss to P/L	50,000		30,000	
		Charge to P/L	90,000	

"You see, Phil, the issue is – do you tell your shareholders about money you've already spent in one year or do you spread it over three years? Whatever you do, it doesn't change the fact that the money was spent three years ago and the only difference as a result of the decision to close is £40,000."

She adds to the cash flow on the other side of the board:

Year	1	2	3	Total
Labour	+ 172	+ 172	+ 172	+ 516
Redundancy	− 45			− 45
Equipment	+ 40			+ 40

I'm still uneasy about this so I say again, "But I can't ignore that £50,000 loss, Chris. It will affect the profit this year and we've not budgeted for it."

"OK. You may feel you want to take it into account because you're profit accountable. But the reality is that the money's gone. Managmeent accounting looks forward and says, on economic grounds, forget it. If you take it into account, it's because of the political impact on this year's profit. You'll benefit in future years because the depreciation will no longer be charged."

I see what she means – our thinking in the past has never looked forward in this way. I remember Appleby telling us we couldn't sell a machine that was useless to us because the book loss was too much for us to bear. We all agreed, particularly Jim, who was pleased not to have to. explain it to Prior. But it was economic nonsense. We should have taken the cash flow from selling it and saved the space in the factory.

Meanwhile Chris has written up some more figures:

Year	1	2	3	Total
Labour	+ 172	+ 172	+ 172	+ 516
Redundancy	− 45			− 45
Equipment	+ 40			+ 40
Food costs	+ 208	+ 208	+ 208	+ 624
Crockery/cutlery	+ 7	+ 7	+ 7	+ 21
Other expenses	+ 11.5	+ 11.5	+ 11.5	+ 34.5

"Remember what we're doing," she says. " This is the cash flow effect of closure. And all the costs I've entered seem to be avoidable."

"Avoidable? What does that mean?"

"What it sounds like. You can avoid it. It can be saved, in cash, if we close the department. I've got to make some more enquiries to see if there is any further cash flow effect because of food stocks, but we'll certainly save £208,000 costs each year."

"What about inflation?"

"That's a good point, but I'm deliberately leaving it out. The quote from the caterers is subject to increase with inflation so I'm ignoring it on both sides."

"You've forgotten the manager's salary."

"No, I haven't. It isn't avoidable. There's no cash flow saving. Didn't George Dixon tell you what's happening to Pete the Catering Manager?"

"Yes, we're keeping him on as Services Manager. I've agreed to that. George is always a bit thinly spread in his department and he'll need someone to manage the contract."

"You wouldn't have made the appointment otherwise, would you?"

"No."

"So there's no cash flow change. Pete will be paid just the same as before".

"Is that why you've left out central indirects too?"

"Yes. We don't save them. I've included other expenses because they are specific to the department and I've checked that they're all avoidable."

"Good, I'm getting the idea. That's the total cash flow effect then?"

"It is. I've just got to include the cash paid out to the caterers – £365,000 each year."

Again I feel excitement and anticipation.

This positive, forward-looking way of presenting the figures actually makes you more interested. Future cash flow seems so much more real than past costs. Chris writes the final amounts in and adds up the columns.

Year	I	2	3	Total
Labour	+ 172	+ 172	+ 172	+ 516
Redundancy	− 45			− 45
Equipment	+ 40			+ 40
Food costs	+ 208	+ 208	+ 208	+ 624
Crockery/cutlery	+ 7	+ 7	+ 7	+ 21
Other expenses	+ 11.5	+ 11.5	+ 11.5	+ 34.5
Favourable cash flows	+ 393.5	+ 398.5	+ 398.'	+ 1,190.5
Contract	− 365.0	− 365.0	− 365.0	− 1,095.0
Net effect	+ 28.5	+ 33.5	+ 33.5	+ 95.5

"That's much closer," I say. "We only save £28,500 in the first year."

"And you have the embarrassment of the book loss of £50,000 on the equipment," Chris points out.

"I thought you said I should ignore that," I say with a smile.

"You should," she replies, "but I was being realistic. Prior may not think in cash flow terms even if we do."

"I'm not sure that we should go through all the hassle of subcontracting just for about £30,000 a year," I say. "What do you think?"

"On pure financial grounds you should close. Only you can weigh the hassle factor against the financial result. But what about the other side of that? Won't it save a lot of management time if we subcontract? We're not in the catering business after all, are we?"

I take her point but all my instincts turn me towards no change. Yet I'm still concerned that the subcontractors can do it so much more cheaply and make a profit. I mention this to Chris.

"OK," she says, "why not tell George and Pete they've got to bring their own costs down? Let's try and find out why our costs are so high. If we can save £30,000 a year on existing operations, we'd be better off in-house anyway.

If you like, I'll do some analysis of their costs over the last few years."

"Yes, and how about some cost per meal figures?" I say. "I've a feeling that subcontracting is George Dixon's easy answer to a management problem. I'll tell him that I won't recommend subcontracting to the management meeting but I want to hear how he's going to bring down his costs by at lest 10 per cent."

"Why 10 per cent?"

"That's the figure MDs always use. Don't they say that it's the best method of cost reduction? The boss's 10 per cent edict?"

"That's too arbitrary, Phil. Let me do some analysis to gauge the likely cost reduction potential. Then we'll decide on a figure."

"Fine," I say, "my only concern is that George and Pete may not be committed to the idea. They were both strongly in favour of subcontracting."

"Because they're both guaranteed a job," Chris says. "The rest of the staff won't feel the same if they're going to be made redundant."

"Then I'll speak to the rest of the staff," I say, "and tell them that we're not going to subcontract for the time being but that, unless costs can be brought down, we may have to do so in the future. That'll put pressure on George and Pete to do something about the costs."

I feel pleased about this discussion. I'm beginning to see that, in my role as MD, the financial evaluations present only one aspect of the decision. I have to balance all the other factors. Also, as in this case, further financial analysis can focus management action in the right area. The cost reductions, when they come, will be informed, not arbitrary.

I sit back and see that it's just gone midday. I have a lunch appointment with an important client at one o'clock. On an impulse I say, "Would my management accountant like a glass of sherry? One of the fringe benefit of being acting MD is that I have a cocktail cabinet."

"I'd love one, please Mr MD," she answers with a smile. "I can tell you enjoy this power and all the trappings that go with it."

"I do, Chris. I must admit that I've never enjoyed my work so much. It's going to be tough when Jim comes back."

"If he does."

I walk over to the cocktail cabinet and pour her a sherry. She smiles sweetly at me as she takes it and it makes me feel weak at the knees. Middle-aged managing directors shouldn't feel this way, but I do.

She settles down in one of the easy chairs and I sit opposite her.

"What do you think of Ames? I ask, "I hear you spent some time with him discussing the budget."

She gives me a concerned look and says, "You didn't mind, did you?"

"Of course not." I wish I meant it.

"I like him," she says and my heart sinks. "He's young, very bright and I'm sure he'll be good for us. His financial background will be very useful at management meetings. But somehow he doesn't seem broad enough for an MD. Still sees the financial aspects as most important. I may be biased but I'd rather have you." She smiles hesitantly and looks embarrassed. "I shouldn't really be talking like this to you. Please forgive me if I'm speaking out of turn."

"No, not at all, Chris. I like talking to you. I feel I can be open with you. And with this job you need someone to talk to, someone who'll tell you what you need to hear. So please don't stop. I just hope that Prior and the others at Universal agree with you. The timing of Jim's accident has made it all very interesting. Much as I regret the circumstances, it's given me a much stronger chance. I'm in the driving seat."

We sip our drinks quietly for a while. Chris breaks the silence with a new subject.

"I was sorry to hear about your daughter, Phil. Is that the one who likes horses?"

"Yes. I've only got one daughter. My son Mark's only ten and prefers football to horses."

"How is she?"

"A lot better now we've talked it through. It all seems to stem from the break up of our marriage. But it has brought Jean and me much closer. Last weekend the family were all together for the first time since we split up and it felt great. I'm hoping now we can have a civilized relationship as parents – it'll be so much easier for the children. The bitterness between us is really what caused the problem with Angie."

"So I guess it's not a good time for me to take her riding."

"Not really, Chris, thanks all the same. Maybe in a few months' time."

"But I may not..."

She stops suddenly.

"What were you going to say, Chris, you may not what?"

"It's not certain but I may not be here. I've been meaning to mention it – I've applied for an MBA course at Harvard. I didn't think I had a chance when I applied but I have an interview in about ten days' time. I'm sorry to spring it on you but you might as well be prepared if I do get the place. It would mean leaving in about six months."

She's sorry! I wonder how sorry she'd be if she knew how I feel at the thought of her leaving?

Insecurity at the thought of losing her help with the financial issues. Disappointment at the thought of no longer having her to confide in. And despair just at the thought of her not being around.

Chapter 14

I'm standing in the bread department with Appleby, watching the freshly sliced and packed loaves move remorselessly along the motorized conveyor belt. He's trying, above all the noise of the machinery around us, to tell me how a new custom-built piece of machinery will save three operatives on the bread slicing and packing line. It will also increase volume of throughput and enable us to sell more sliced loaves, which are currently restricted by our production capacity.

I haven't a clue about the technical aspects and, even if I could hear what he's saying above the noise, I almost certainly wouldn't understand it. And neither would Jim if he were here. You employ people like Appleby to deal with the technical side, but an MD is expected at least to listen to their complex explanations.

"I know it's only got a five-year payback," he says, "but the DCF rate of return is over 20 per cent if you assume a ten-year life. So I reckon it's worth doing, don't you?"

I can still hardly hear his voice over the noise of the machinery so I beckon him to move into the relative quiet of his office.

"The problem is," he continues, still shouting although now he doesn't need to, "that Prior is still hooked on payback and doesn't really look at DCF's. I wonder if he understands it. The Group Accountants look at the DCF rate of return, but it's Prior and the board who make the decision."

I ask a safe question to conceal the fact that I don't know

what he's talking about. "What payback does Prior look for?"

"Three years," replies Appleby, "and all he's doing by that is pushing us into more and more short-term projects. DCF looks at projects much more long-term. I think that's one of its main advantages, don't you?"

One of the advantages of being the MD is that you can change the subject when you want to. I ignore his comment and follow my own path.

"Who's doing the project appraisal calculations now?"

"Chris Goodhart. She's totally with me on this. She's appalled by the Group emphasis on short-term payback."

I escape quickly before it becomes clear how far I am out of my depth. I go straight back to my office and ring Chris. I don't mind admitting my ignorance of financial matters to her but I don't want to be exposed by Appleby again. And, being acting MD, I can now quite legitimately ask Chris to give her time to help me.

Not that I need to pull rank. She seems to have forgotten her earlier reluctance to carry on the evening meetings and agrees to see me about six. It gives me a warm feeling to think we are back to our evening tutorials again. I haven't seen her in the week since she told me that she might be going to the States and, after the initial shock, I have tended to put it out of my mind, thinking that it might not happen. My disappointment at the news was not just at the personal level. The idea of working at Lawrensons, particularly as MD, and not having her to help with financial advice, is not at all appealing. Who else could help me out of the sort of embarrassing experience I've just had with Appleby?

For a while I fantasized about following her to the States and even getting a job over there. But then I thought of my commitments, particularly of my children, whom I couldn't possibly leave as things are at present. I do have the worst of all worlds. The girl I care about is going away. And though I no longer have the family pleasures which used to mean so much, my wife and children are still my responsibility. Still, I mustn't feel sorry for myself. The job is going well. The Kwikmart own-label deal has been agreed, and Prior has formally accepted the budget. And the latest news on sales volume is that trends are up on latest estimates, so this year's profits may be even better than we thought. Malcolm reckons that my trips to visit the sales force helped morale a lot and may be connected with the increase. I don't much care why – I'm just glad it's happened and Prior, on his weekly visit yesterday, continued to show that he's impressed. If only I could achieve the same success in my private life.

Before Chris comes to see me, I have a look at Jim's file of capital proposals. I've seen these at board meetings before but never looked at them properly. I pull out a recent one for a new mixing machine in the cake department. There's some data about the machine, its make, how much it costs and some narrative explanations about why it was purchased and what savings it will make. In this case the savings were a combination of reduced labour costs and some improvements in material yield. I turn to the two appendices – technical and financial. The technical one contains the machine's technical specification and is, I suppose, for the Universal Group Technical Director to check on Appleby's assumptions. The financial appendix contains a mass of figures with the initial investment, savings for each of the ten years split between labour and materials and an extra line called residual values. I make a mental note to ask Chris about that. Then, at the bottom of the page, I find what I've been looking for. Three boxes which say:

Payback	4.2 years
NPV (13%)	+ 62.1
DCF rate of return	18.2%

I think I know what payback means because I've used that in my personal life to evaluate whether to invest in double glazing and cavity wall insulation – how long does it take to recover the initial investment? That's what Appleby was referring to. The DCF rate of return was the other method he talked about which apparently he and all the other

accountants believe in but Prior and the board appear to
·ignore. But NPV is new to me, so I can ask Chris about
this too.

She comes in at six with her computer.

"I may want to do some sensitivity analysis for you," she
says.

"I think I need some basic explanations before we get
on to the computer," I reply. "Appleby's been blinding me
with science and I don't like it. And looking at the capital
proposal file, I've found even more accounting gobbledegook
– DCFs, NPVs. Why can't you accountants use English like
everyone else?"

She smiles, knowing that I'm only pulling her leg. I can
tell that she gets real job satisfaction from helping poor non-
numerate idiots like me to break through the jargon.

"I'll try, Phil. It isn't really as complex as people think,
but the mathematical basis behind DCF does need careful
explanation."

"Can you use the figures that Appleby's putting into the
slicing and packing machinery project?"

"I will later but I'd rather use some more basic data at
first. Let me put some figures on the board." She writes
up:

	Project A	Project B
Investment	10,000	10,000
Return		
Year 1	+ 1,000	+ 5,000
Year 2	+ 2,000	+ 4,000
Year 3	+ 3,000	+ 3,000
Year 4	+ 4,000	+ 1,000
Year 5	+ 5,000	+ 1,000
Total return	+ 15,000	+ 14,000
Profit	5,000	4,000

"OK," she says, "which project would you go for?"

"I should think B," I reply, seizing the chance to show my knowledge of at least one concept. "The payback's better, quite good, in fact, at 2.5 years. The other one's much longer – 4 years."

I feel quite clever, having carried out that feat of simple arithmetic which would just about have got me through my primary school exam. And Chris adds to my self-satisfaction by saying, "Well done. At least you understand payback, like most people at Universal. The trouble is – that's all they take into account. Can you see how payback can be a limited method of deciding between two investments?"

"Well, Project A makes more profit so I suppose that must be important too."

"Yes," she says, "though I'll show you a bit later how, in present value terms, it's worth less than it seems. But also Project A could make enormous profits in Year 5 and thereafter. Say it made 100,000 in Year 5 rather than 5,000, you would perhaps wonder if payback gives you the right decision, wouldn't you?"

"Yes, I see what you mean. And I see what Appleby meant when he said that payback doesn't look at the longer term. It just looks for your money back and doesn't look for profit."

"Absolutely, though that doesn't mean that it should be rejected altogether. It just means it has limitations on its own. Can you see any other limitations?"

I can't so I just shake my head, feeling guilty at my ignorance.

"Well," says Chris, "it isn't a payback in real terms, is it?"

Another look at the figures makes me appreciate what should have been pretty obvious. If I lent somebody £10,000 and they paid me back over two and a half years, I'd want some interest. The payback must really be longer than that if the interest is to be repaid too.

"Don't you see," she carries on, "the problem with payback and with trying to calculate a profit from future cash flows is that you're trying to relate money in the future to money today. But money in the future must be worth less in present value terms, mustn't it? That's why the £5,000 profit from A can't be compared with the £4,000 from B. Project A has its best return in Year 5, when it earns £5,000. But this must be worth less than the £5,000 which B earns in Year 1. Do you see the point, Phil, because it's fundamental to DCF? Money in the future is worth less in real terms than money today."

I feel like saying, "Do you think I'm stupid or something?", because it seems obvious that money is worth more today than it is in the future. But she's trying so hard, giving up her evening once again to help me, that I restrain myself. In any case, after the earlier demonstrations of my ignorance, she probably has good reason to doubt my mental capacity.

"Now," she says, turning to another part of the whiteboard, "this next part is particularly important so please try to concentrate – I know it's hard after a long day."

"Yes, teacher," I say with a smile and my reward is a smile in return. However hard I try, I just can't forget the hold this girl has over me, but I take notice of what she says and make a special effort to concentrate. I'm determined to understand DCF and badly want to be able to talk to people like Appleby without having to bluff it out.

"OK," she continues, "would you rather have £100 now or £100 in a year's time?"

"£100 now, of course."

"Why? I know it may seem obvious but tell me why?"

"Because I can invest it if I have it now."

"Assuming you have surplus funds and that you would invest it."

"Yes," I say, "I see what you mean. In fact, with my commitments, I don't have surplus funds and the hundred pounds would just go to reduce my overdraft."

"That's right. But you'd save yourself interest so the money now is still worth more than having it in a year's time."

I nod my head, feeling again that she's underestimating my knowledge and basic intelligence.

"OK", she says, "so, in principle, it doesn't matter if you're in surplus or in deficit, you'd still be better off having the £100 now rather than in a year's time. Let's just assume for the moment that you have surplus funds and that you can gain 10 per cent by investing them. It's easier to see it that way, I think."

She writes on the board:

Year 0	100
Year 1	110
	Rate 10 per cent

"What does year 0 mean? I ask.

"It's often used in investment projects," she replies. "It's today, the immediate outlay, whereas Year 1 is one year from now. OK?"

I nod and she carries on, as enthusiastic as ever, determined to make me understand, whether I like it or not.

"Now," she says, "we're assuming you have £100 today, you can invest it and make it into £110 in a year's time. Let's turn it round another way. Assuming you can earn 10 per cent by investing, what would you accept today instead of £100 in a year's time?"

I let this sink in. One hundred pounds in a year's time. I should obviously accept less today because I can invest it. I should accept £90. No, that would only make £99 at 10 per cent. So it must be just over £90–£91 near enough.

"£91", I call out, quite pleased at this piece of mathematics which in my schooldays I would have walked through. How the brain becomes rusty in the non-numerate world of sales and marketing management.

"OK then. What you're saying is that £91 is the present value of £100 in a year's time, assuming a rate of 10 per cent." She writes up:

Year 0	100	91 = Present value
Year 1	110	100
Rate	10%	10%

"You arrived at that £91 by a bit of mathematical logic and trial and error, right? Well, you can also get to it by the process of discounting which is the basic concept behind DCF."

She writes up:

$$100 \times \frac{100}{110} = 91$$

"If 100 makes 110 in a year's time, the figure which makes 100 will be reduced by the ratio of 100 to 110. That's what discounting means, converting future amounts to their present value, what they're worth today. You do this by discount factors. Let me show you."

She writes up:

Year 0	1.00
Year 1	$0.91 \left(1.00 \times \frac{100}{110}\right)$
Year 2	$0.83 \left(0.91 \times \frac{100}{110}\right)$
Year 3	$0.75 \left(0.83 \times \frac{100}{110}\right)$

"I'm now working in units of £1 rather than £100," she says, "so, instead of £91, I've put the present value of £1 in a year's time as £0.91, or 91 pence. And you continue the discounting process into the future so that the present value of £1 in two years' time is 0.83 and in three years' time 0.75. Can you grasp what this means?"

It means that if I have 75p now, I could invest it at 10 per cent and make it into £1 in three years' time. Thus that £1 in three years' time is worth 75p today. Discounting is the way of working back to that figure – really it's compounding upside down. I mention this to Chris.

"Yes," she says, "exactly right. That's all discounting is. A way of converting future money into its present value today."

"But I'm not sure how it helps me as a manager."

"You'll see in a minute, Phil. Just think back to Project A and Project B. The main problem was relating monies coming back in the future to an investment today. Now we have a way of converting them all to the same value, their present value. Let's look at the two projects after they've been discounted."

		Project A			Project B	
	Discount factor at 10%	Present value		Discount factor at 10%	Present value	
Year 0 − 10,000	1.00	− 10,000	− 10,000	1.00	− 10,000	
Year 1 + 1,000	0.91	+ 910	+ 5,000	0.91	+ 4,550	
Year 2 + 2,000	0.83	+ 1,660	+ 4,000	0.83	+ 3,320	
Year 3 + 3,000	0.75	+ 2,250	+ 3,000	0.75	+ 2,250	
Year 4 + 4,000	0.68	+ 2,720	+ 1,000	0.68	+ 680	
Year 5 + 5,000	0.62	+ 3,100	+ 1,000	0.62	+ 620	
Total + 5,000		+ 640	+ 4,000		+ 1,420	

She writes these up one by one explaining as she goes. The £1,000 in Year 1 for Project A is multiplied by 0.91 to convert to a present value of £910. Yet the £1,000 in Year 5 for Project B is multiplied by 0.62 to arrive at £620, because you have to wait that much longer for it. It's common sense really. All it shows is that, the longer you wait for money, the less it's worth. And this method shows that Project B is better than Project A after converting to present values, mainly because its best years were early on when it had a higher weighting than Project A, whose best return was in Year 5.

Chris is watching me study the figures.

"Do you get the idea?" she asks, looking concerned.

"I believe I do. You're just converting all the future monies into what they're worth today and the one with the highest return in present value terms is the best."

"That's right," she says and adds with a smile. "Do you know what those final figures of +640 and +1,420 are called?"

I shake my head.

"Net present value. The net amount of cash in present value terms after the initial investment has been covered."

"So?"

"What are the initials of net present value?"

"Of course – NPV! That's what was on the capital proposal form. I see."

"But what do you think it means in management terms, in the context of this decision?"

"That B is better than A."

"Yes. That's true but, if we just take B, what does it mean?"

"That it's worth doing."

"Right. It's better than doing nothing because you've got your money back and some extra cash in present value terms."

"If it's positive you can go ahead."

"You might not necessarily go ahead. There's the question of risk and of other projects which might make more money. That's why there's a second measure, the DCF rate of return. NPV carries you over the first hurdle. If you've understood this, can we move to the DCF rate of return?"

"Yes," I reply, "but before we do, what about the rate? How do you decide on that? We've just taken 10 per cent. Surely the rate is critical, because all the present values would be different at different rates, wouldn't they?"

"Yes, they would and you'll see that more clearly in a minute. The answer to your question is that each company has to fix its own rate based on its financial circumstances. If you have surplus funds, the rate would be what you can get by investing elsewhere because that's what you are giving up by investing in the project. If you're borrowing the money to invest, the rate would be the company's cost of capital. That can be a very complicated calculation because there are various forms of capital all with different rates, but all you really need to know is that Universal give us their cost of capital figure to use and that's 13 per cent."

I'm glad she's not going to take me into any more complexity because, after thinking I was being patronized, I'm now struggling to keep up. And now she changes up yet another gear.

"Now let's turn to the DCF rate of return. I'll use the computer because it will save us time. Let's concentrate solely on Project B, OK?"

She types in a few entries and I see the figures for Project B on the screen.

"OK," she says, "you agree that the net present value of £1,420 for Project B is only that figure because we assumed 10 per cent?"

I nod in agreement.

"And that other rates would give different NPV's?"

I nod again.

"And that if we try long enough we must get a figure that gives us breakeven?"

"What do you mean by breakeven?" I ask.

I try to avoid looking at her as she walks over to the whiteboard because I really want to concentrate on what she's saying. But the grace of her movements and the attractions of her face and figure make this even more difficult than usual. It's also gone seven o'clock and I'm tired and hungry, but I make a great effort to keep up my concentration. She rubs off some of the figures and writes up:

Project B	10%	$x\%$
Initial investment	$-10,000$	$-10,000$
Present values of cash inflows	$+11,420$	$+10,000$
Net present value	$+1,420$	$-$

"You see, Phil. There must somewhere be a rate which brings the cash inflows back to £10,000 and gives a net present value of zero. That's the DCF rate of return."

"How do you calculate it?"

"By trial and error. There's no perfect mathematical formula. The computer can work it out at the press of a button but, even there, the programme has to try different rates and then home in on the DCF rate of return. I've programmed it to show all the NPV calculations at a few different rates so you can see what happens."

She presses a few buttons and I look at the screen. The first set of figures shows Project B at 20 per cent.

		Discount Factor at 20%	Present Value	
Year 0	− 10,000	1.00	− 10,000	
Year 1	+ 5,000	0.83	+ 4,150	
Year 2	+ 4,000	0.69	+ 2,760	
Year 3	+ 3,000	0.58	+ 1,740	
Year 4	+ 1,000	0.48	+ 480	
Year 5	+ 1,000	0.40	+ 400	
Total	+ 4,000		− 470	Net present value

"What does that tell us?" she asks.

"That 20 per cent is too high," I reply. "We only get 9,530 back after investing 10,000, so there's a negative NPV of 470. Can you call it a negative NPV?"

She nods and then says, "OK. We lose money at 20 per cent so that rate is too high. The breakeven rate is below that. Can you see roughly where the DCF rate of return will fall?"

We've a positive NPV of 1,420 at 10 per cent and a negative of 470 at 20 per cent, a total range of 1,890. So the breakeven must be nearer to 20 per cent than 10 per cent, probably somewhere between 17 and 18 per cent. When I suggest this to Chris she seems delighted. She presses some more keys on the computer and the figures come up discounted at 17 per cent:

		Discount Factor at 17%	Present Value	
Year 0	− 10,000	1.00	− 10,000	
Year 1	+ 5,000	0.85	+ 4,250	
Year 2	+ 4,000	0.73	+ 2,920	
Year 3	+ 3,000	0.62	+ 1,860	
Year 4	+ 1,000	0.53	+ 530	
Year 5	+ 1,000	0.46	+ 460	
Total	+ 4,000		+ 20	Net present value

"That seems just about it," she says. "I'll try 18 per cent but I think it will be further away from breakeven and it's not worth trying to be more accurate than to the nearest 1 per cent."

She brings up the figures at 18 per cent:

		Discount Factor at 18%	Present Value	
Year 0	− 10,000	1.00	− 10,000	
Year 1	+ 5,000	0.85	+ 4,250	
Year 2	+ 4,000	0.72	+ 2,880	
Year 3	+ 3,000	0.61	+ 1,830	
Year 4	+ 1,000	0.52	+ 520	
Year 5	+ 1,000	0.44	+ 440	Net
Total	+ 4,000		− 80	present value

"Yes, it's 17 per cent near enough. It's £20 away from breakeven at 17 per cent but £80 at 18 per cent. Now it's important to understand what this means. Can you remember what it's called?"

"The breakeven rate?"

"That's what it really is, but Universal's name for it is DCF rate of return – you remember seeing that on the capital proposal. There are other names which are often used – DCF yield is one and computers often label it the internal rate of return or IRR. But more important is what it means to you as a manager. Can you see what it tells you?"

I look at the figures again. "I suppose it means that we could still break even if the interest rates went as high as 18 per cent. Is that right?"

"Absolutely, Phil. That's excellent – you've understood it exactly. And it also means that we have an 8 per cent safety margin over our original rate of 10 per cent to cover the risk of the project. This gives us a financial indicator which we can use to weigh against the special risk factors and to compare with other projects. It provides a means of ranking projects and relating them to each other."

"Does it mean that we're making 18 per cent on the project? Can I think in those terms?"

"Yes, in a way. Because, if you can break even while paying 18 per cent interest, you must be making an 18 per cent return before interest throughout the project, mustn't you?"

I'm still struggling to grasp all she's saying but I think I've got the general idea. Now I tell Chris I need to see it happen on an actual project like the bread packing machinery.

"Yes," she says, "and you can see the sensitivities too. That's a very powerful way of using the DCF rate of return."

"What do you mean by sensitivities? You mentioned it before but I wasn't sure what you were getting at."

"Just asking 'what if?' questions as we did when we looked at the product mix options soon after I first came here. Once we've put the basic cash flows into the computer, we can change the assumptions and see what effects that has on the DCF rate of return."

"What do you mean by cash flows?" I ask.

"Remember when we looked at the catering subcontracting. It's the actual effect on the bank account. All the cash benefits which will happen directly as a result of the investment."

Now, how does this apply to Appleby's machinery? He mentioned that there were labour savings but also extra volume. Chris brings the cash flows for the project out of a file. She tells me that the cash flows she'd agreed with Appleby are based on saving three operatives and the extra contribution from increasing sliced bread sales by 5 per cent. This is the volume we're losing at present because we're not producing enough to meet our customers' needs.

Even though it's getting late, I'm sufficiently interested to carry on and Chris says she doesn't mind. I hope she's not saying it just because I'm the boss at the moment, but she does seem genuinely pleased that I've grasped the principle of DCF.

She takes me through all the cash flows. The savings on operative labour are fairly straightforward. Apparently they can be achieved through natural wastage, so there will be no costs or problems of redundancy. She then shows me how she's included the extra sales less variable costs and a few other extra costs caused by the new machinery, particularly the cost of a new maintenance contract. She also shows me how she's built in an assumed residual value of the machinery at the end of the project. Apparently Universal ask for all projects to be cut off after ten years, and Appleby has projected an estimate of resale value at the end of that time.

I ask Chris how she can be sure Appleby isn't quoting optimistic figures just to get his case through.

"You can never be sure but at least you can ask the right questions to test him out. You might do that with him some time and then you can judge how well he's thought it through. I've already done that with some of the cash flows on this project and he seems to have done his homework."

"Did you check the resale value of his plant?"

"No, because it's not that sensitive to the overall outcome. Let me show you what happens to the return when we take the resale value out altogether."

She brings up some more figures on the computer screen. It's a cash flow summary of the bread packing machinery project. She enters zero in the residual value column for the final year and presses a key.

"There, you see. The DCF rate of return was just over 20 per cent and now it's just under, so it's hardly changed at all. That's not one of the most sensitive assumptions."

"What is, then?"

"The extra sales volume. Let me show you. If we only achieve a 4 per cent volume increase rather than 5 per cent, the return of 20 per cent comes down to 15 per cent. Or at least I think that's what I worked out yesterday."

She enters a few figures and the sensitivity is confirmed. One per cent less sales volume and we're down to 15 per cent return, 2 per cent less and the return is only 10 per cent, below Universal's cost of capital of 13 per cent. I ask her to test the sensitivity of the labour savings. She enters some more figures and tells me, "Not quite so sensitive. If we only save two operatives rather than the three we've assumed, the return comes down to 18 per cent. Volume is the important one to check."

I'm beginning to see just what DCF can do, particularly when there's someone like Chris to quantify the effect of changes and a computer to do the number crunching.

"Chris," I say, "can you bring your machine in tomorrow afternoon when I have my regular weekly meeting with Appleby? I'd like to test him out as you suggested. I'll see Malcolm about the sales position – I want to be sure that we can get his extra volume."

The next afternoon I begin to see the power of management accounting. I go through all the assumptions with Appleby. I've already checked with Malcolm and he's confirmed that the sales are there as long as Appleby can produce. I ask Appleby how sure he is of his production volumes and his staff savings. Chris shows him the calculations we did and he expresses surprise at the sensitivity to volume. But he assures me that his cash flow assumptions are valid and I believe him.

I can see he's surprised and, I suspect, impressed by the way the proposal has been analysed. He even says that Universal ought to ask for some sensitivity analysis rather than just asking for the normal indicators. I say I'll support the project despite the long payback by Universal standards. I now feel confident to argue the case with Prior. I'm even looking forward to showing him my new knowledge of DCF, particularly if, as Appleby believes, he doesn't fully understand it himself. Appleby leaves my office and Chris stays.

"I've got a draft of your new management information report, Phil. Can I show it to you?"

I'm pretty exhausted but don't want to upset her.

"All right," I say, but then Sylvia comes into the room, looking flustered and embarrassed.

"Mr Moorley," she says, "you have two visitors."

"Have they an appointment, Sylvia? I can't remember seeing one in my diary."

"No, Mr Moorley, but can I speak to you privately?"

"Let me come and speak to them, Sylvia."

I walk to my door and see them sitting in the outer office.

"Oh," I say, "you two. What on earth are you doing here?

I suppose you'd better come in."

They come in and Chris is still sitting at my table. She looks up.

"Chris, how would you like to meet my children? Angela, Mark, this is Christine, my management accountant."

Chapter 15

Chris stays to chat with the kids for five minutes. They seem relaxed, not at all embarrassed, despite coming to Lawrensons for the first time in five years, completely unannounced. Angela seems much the way she used to be before her truancy and chats away about her riding lessons. Marks sits on my chair, rocking and spinning round, just as he used to as a little boy in my own, smaller office all those years ago.

Chris has a way with children, not talking down but showing a genuine interest in them. She senses when it's time to leave and I'm left alone with my offspring: Mark, ten, tousle-haired and mischievous, Angela, three years older, maturing into an attractive teenager, beginning to look like her mother.

"Well," I say, "what's all this about? Does your Mum know you're here?"

"No," says Mark. "This is a smashing office, Dad. Are you going to keep it?"

"No. It's only temporary while Mr Lawrence is away. Don't change the subject. You shouldn't be here without telling your Mum. I'd better phone her."

"There's no point, Dad," says Angela. "She's gone out for the evening and we're staying with Auntie Susan."

Susan is an old family friend whom I haven't seen for years but I know she's still very close to Jean.

"Does Auntie Susan know where you are?"

"Yes. She dropped us off here and promised to pick us up at seven." Susan always was an interferer although she was usually well-intentioned. I wonder if she's put the children up to this? As if reading my mind, Angela says, "This was our idea, Dad. We wanted to talk to you alone and it's difficult now we're spending our weekends together."

"And we do like that, Dad. We've thoroughly enjoyed these last two weekends you've come to our house."

So have I. The only problem has been going back to the flat on Sunday evening and reminding myself that I'm not really a part of the family at all, just someone who's around when things go wrong.

"Well, what do you want to talk about?"

"Well, Dad," says Angela, "it's Mum and you. Mark and I had the feeling when you took us out at weekends that, well. . ."

"That you wouldn't mind coming back to us," says Mark, coming to his sister's rescue.

"And we knew, until the last few months, that Mum wouldn't hear of it. But now we think, since my—er—problems, that she might want you to if you asked her. So we sort of thought you ought to know."

They look so earnest and so hopeful but I don't know how to respond. I can't build up their hopes when I'm not sure of my own feelings or of Jean's. But I mustn't slap them down if I want to keep the better relationship I'm now having with them. "It's good of you to come to see me and I'll think about what you've said. I could discuss it with Mum but it's not something we're going to decide overnight, you know that don't you?"

They nod their heads and look pleased. I'm afraid of building up their hopes too much and so I carry on.

"If we were ever to come back together again, it would have to be for good and we'd both have to be sure. And the problems we had before would have to be sorted out, not forgotten."

"What were the problems, Dad? asks Angela. "Can you tell us?"

My immediate instinct is to say no, but I don't. Why not, I think. Aren't they entitled to know? They're old enough to understand now. So I spend over half an hour telling them about the problems – my commitment to work in the difficult years when they were growing up, which were such a restriction on Jean's freedom. Communications seemed to stop and neither of us was able to start talking again. I'm careful not to blame Jean and, if anything, go the other way, stressing my stubbornness but not hers.

They say very little but they seem absorbed and I can tell from their loving looks that they're glad I've told them. And I have a feeling that they haven't heard it before – Jean never could bring herself to talk about anything which hurt.

I don't want to send them home yet.

"How would you like to ring Auntie Susan and tell her I'm taking you out to dinner?"

"Yes, please," they shout together.

"But on one condition. You promise to tell your mother you came here and what we've talked about. We'll get nowhere unless we're honest with each other – OK?"

"We promise," says Angela, looking at Mark who nods approvingly.

"And I promise that whatever happens between your mother and me, we'll still meet as a family as we have done these last two weekends, assuming your mother still wants to. All right?"

I know it's safe to promise this but I'm glad I don't have to go further. All logic tells me that I should make a bid to get Jean back. All my family feelings point that way. There'll never be a better chance. But deep down there's this nagging feeling that there's something better just around the corner – the possibility of spending my future with a girl who's just come into my life and who's made me feel like never before.

We have a great evening at the local Indian restaurant and I let them have some wine which makes us all feel even better. I drop them off at Susan's about 9.30 and they kiss me goodbye with a warmth and naturalness which I haven't felt since the divorce. I feel happy as I drive home and I think how best I should talk to Jean. I decide to ring tomorrow and ask her to lunch in a day or two.

Two mornings later, I'm in early as usual, about 7.30 – a habit that I've kept regularly since Jim's accident. I see at the top of my in-tray a piece of A4 with a note stuck to the top of it – one of those bits of yellow paper which seem to be everywhere these days. It says:

I didn't realize you were so desperate to avoid seeing your new management information sheet that you'd send your children to interrupt us! Seriously, it was nice to meet them – they're lovely kids. But can we discuss this when you have time? It's only a first draft.

Chris

The paper underneath is shown opposite. I study it closely and all sorts of questions spring to mind.

– Why were pie efficiencies down when Appleby is spending so much on capital and allegedly increasing efficiency?

– Why are there so many shortages and again, why pies? With the department being under-utilized, we should never fail to deliver products to meet our orders. And how much lost sales will that have cost us?

– How can our labour turnover be as high as that? How is it calculated? She might have shown the base figures. And what is the absentee rate a percentage of?

– I knew pie volumes were just down on budget but I'd no idea they were that much down on last year. I'd like to see the graph of how they've moved over the last twelve months.

I pick up the phone to see if Chris is in yet, slightly irritated that this paper leaves out so much. Then I notice one more thing. Apart from the financial summary, there's not one financial indicator. It's all units and percentages. How can a management accountant produce a report with hardly any money figures on it?

I don't really expect Chris to be there yet. But she is.

"I didn't know you started this early," I say.

Month of November
Chief executive's key data

	This month	Last month	Last year	Standard
Production yields				
Bread	94.2%	93.6%	92.9%	98%
Cakes	96.6%	97.2%	95.4%	94%
Pies	87.0%	87.6%	89.2%	90%
Labour efficiencies				
Bread	101.6%	99.8%	97.4%	100%
Cakes	98.4%	100.6%	98.1%	100%
Pies	95.2%	99.1%	98.8%	100%
Shortages (tons)				
Bread	6.8	7.2	9.4	–
Cakes	7.4	8.8	8.1	–
Pies	8.9	5.1	6.2	–
Personnel				
Labour turnover	26.8%	25.1%	22.3%	–
Absentee rate	5.2%	4.1%	3.9%	–
Sales Volume (tons)				Budget
Bread	251	224	249	239
Cakes	164	172	148	158
Pies	139	154	162	141
Total	554	550	559	538
Financial (£'000)				
Sales	8,314	7,918	7,516	8,504
Variable costs	(5,512)	(5,201)	(4,895)	(5,743)
Contribution	2,802	2,717	2,621	2,761
Fixed production	(738)	(700)	(692)	(732)
Profit before fixed ind	2,064	2,017	1,929	2,029
Indirects	(1,846)	(1,859)	(1,869)	(1,854)
Net profit	218	158	60	175

"Well, I know you start at this time and I asked Sylvia to put my new report at the top of your in-tray. I had a feeling you might want to talk to me so I came in early just in case."

"Good", I say, "can you come now?"

"Yes, just give me five minutes. I'm finishing another report I've prepared for you. I think you might find it surprising."

She's in my office within ten minutes. Her unusually early start doesn't seem to affect her manner or her appearance. She's looking smart and attractive – she always seems to choose clothes which show her femininity to the full but are also suitable for work. I can tell from the cut of her suit that she shops in the best stores.

She sits down apprehensively opposite my desk.

"What do you think of it, Phil?"

"My first reaction was not very favourable. It seems to leave lots of questions unanswered. Then I remembered what you said – that a good MI report should lead to further questions and more detail. But I'm not so sure. I like to be able to follow things through and I can't without the data."

"But you're the MD – you should be asking the questions now."

"But whom do I ask?"

"Me, John, Malcolm, Wilf, George, all of us. Your management information should help you to keep us on the ball and to pick out the right issues. Remember that report summarizes what you said were your key success variables."

"I still feel I should be getting more data – I particularly remember saying that I wanted graphs to monitor trends of volume and efficiencies."

"I'm working on that, Phil. I'm moving towards putting all this data on microcomputer each month so you can either access it yourself or I'll produce printouts. This is only the start – I thought you'd find it useful."

I can tell she's upset by my response. This has obviously been her pet project and, first I kept putting her off, now I'm showing doubts about the benefits. She avoids my eyes and, for the first time, I see weakness behind that smooth, efficient exterior. She's feeling piqued, just like a child whose parent is not showing approval after good behaviour. I'm rather irritated by her immature attitude but still feel some warmth towards her because, for a change, she seems so vulnerable. I try to mollify her by asking about the other report.

"Are you sure you want to see it?" she asks sharply.

"Yes, Chris. Now come on, I'm very pleased with what you've done since you've been here. I think the MI sheet is a great start but we need to build on it. Now, let's see your other report. I've got a meeting at nine."

She gets the report out though the atmosphere remains cool.

"It's not that urgent or important," she says. "It's some work I've been doing on customer profitability. It follows up on something you said soon after we met."

"I don't recall. I can't say I'm too bothered about the profits our customers make. That's their problem. All the retailers make higher returns than we do."

Her face drops. I've upset her again. Women! Always so sensitive.

"No," she says, real impatience showing through in her voice for the first time I can remember, "I mean the profit we make from dealing with particular customers. You said that, after all the discounts you give them, the credit terms they take and the costs of delivery and administration, you wondered whether we made any money out of some big customers. Well, I'm trying to tell you. And, by the way, I think you're wrong about understanding the profits which your customers make. I think you ought to look at that too."

It's early in the morning, I'm tired and her icy tone makes me even more irritable. I forget how this girl's helped me and the fact that she's come in early specially for me. Despite, or maybe because of, my feelings for her, I can't help showing my annoyance.

"I really must look through my post before my meeting," I say sharply. Leave the report and I'll try to read it later today."

She glares at me, in anger or disappointment, I'm not sure which. She gets up, says thank you and walks out.

She needed bringing down a peg or to, I say to myself. Just because I relied on her a lot when I was Sales and Marketing Director doesn't mean she can expect me to agree with everything she does now that I'm in the MD's chair. And the MI report was rather half-baked, wasn't it? Or was it me, not being used to the top job, wanting more detail than I should have? Anyway, who cares? She's probably going off to the States anyway. Yet I do care and I'll have to make it up with her before too long.

My eyes stray down to the report she's left. Its title is:

FAREPRICE
CUSTOMER PROFITABILITY STATEMENT
FIRST SIX MONTHS

Fareprice
Customer profitability statement
First six months

Sales (list price)		2,184,792	100.0
Discounts – Cash	–		
Quantity	48,924		(2.2)
Special	264,165		(12.1)
		313,089	
Sales (net)		1,871,703	85.7
Variable production costs		1,343,521	(61.5)
Contribution		528,182	24.2
Fixed production costs		182,110	(8.4)
Gross profit		346,072	15.8
Customer direct costs			
– Selling	54,860		(2.5)
– Sales administration	24,113		(1.1)
– Distribution	118,246		(5.4)
– Special merchandizing	6,815		(0.3)
– Interest on working capital	49,501		(2.3)
		253,535	
Customer contribution		92,537	4.2
Apportionment of general indirects		124,817	(5.7)
Net loss		(32,280)	(1.5)

Fareprice are one of our top five customers, a leading multiple chain, owned by a large aggressive holding company. They don't sell own-brand and are therefore an attractive customer, but they do negotiate very competitively on price. They also require a lot of sales attention and ask for frequent deliveries to their regional depots, in order to keep their stocks as low as possible. They are also one of the worst payers – we're always having to press them to settle their account. But they give us regular volume of branded goods.

I look down the report and can't quite believe what I see.

Can this be true? Are we actually losing money on Fareprice? No wonder Chris wanted me to see it. I move to telephone her but then think not. Mustn't appear to be wanting to build that bridge too quickly. I can make it up with her later. Make it up? Don't be silly, Moorley, you're her boss, she's the accountant. If only it were that simple. If only my feelings towards her were rational, business-related ones.

Instead I phone Malcolm and arrange to see him mid-morning, after my early meeting. I ask him to bring his Fareprice file with him. I wonder if Chris has involved him in the evaluation as she has on previous occasions?

I soon find out that she hasn't. When I show Malcolm the figures, his eyes widen and, unusually for him, he frowns.

"Who's produced this, Phil? It's absolute rubbish. I've been looking after Fareprice personally for six years and now you tell me we're losing on it. I'd like to see where those cost apportionments come from. There's no way we're going to save that amount of costs if we lose Fareprice's business."

Chris told me about avoidable costs when we were discussing the catering subcontracting. Malcolm is saying that most of these costs, particularly those at the bottom of the statement, are not avoidable. Yet Chris has included them in this evaluation.

I wonder if I've been wrong about her? Is she not quite as competent and professional as she makes out? She's being inconsistent, telling us to ignore cost apportionments for one evaluation, then including them for the next.

Just then the phone rings. It's Sylvia.

"Miss Goodhart's on the line, Mr Moorley. I told her

you were with Mr Davies but she was quite insistent."

I decide not to tell her I'll ring back. At least she's made the first move.

"Hello," says that familiar voice, sounding, for a change, a little hesitant, "I'm sorry to interrupt and I'm sorry about this morning. It was early and I was a little frustrated that I couldn't get the reaction I wanted from the MI sheet."

She hurries on, almost as if she doesn't want to hear my reply.

"But I saw Malcolm going into your office and I've been very worried that you've been discussing the Fareprice customer profitability statement. Have you?"

"Yes, we have actually. Wasn't that what we were supposed to do?"

Again I find myself getting slightly irritated with her. Why shouldn't I discuss it with Malcolm if I want to? I wish I knew why she's suddenly begun to make me feel like this. Maybe she's been a bit too perfect up to now.

"Yes," she says, ignoring my sharpness, "but I would like to have explained its purpose and its context first. It can be dangerous to use this sort of statement in the wrong way and it can create misunderstandings. Any chance of my joining you?"

My irritation with her is overcome by a belief that she will contribute to our discussion and that she should have the chance to explain the figures before Malcolm and I go too far in our conclusions.

"All right. Come straight away."

In the few minutes that it takes for her to arrive, I tell Malcolm what she said about wanting to explain the purpose. This doesn't mollify him – he still seems defensive and annoyed about the implications of the figures.

She comes in and sits next to Malcolm and me in the leather chairs in the far corner of the office. She smiles at Malcolm but he looks away. Then she smiles at me, almost pleadingly, I feel. Again her vulnerability and my underlying feelings take over. Whatever she does, it's going to be very difficult for me to stay annoyed with her for long.

"All right, Chris," I say, "tell us about this statement. What made you decide to do it?"

"Well, I first saw it in Universal. The Internal Consultancy Division recommended customer profitability analysis systems for all our companies supplying the retail trade a few years ago and I was sent into two companies to help implement it."

"Why haven't we got the system then?" asks Malcolm. "We supply the retail trade."

"I don't know, Malcolm. It was a circular which the Group Accountant sent to all Managing Directors. But it wasn't mandatory so I suppose no-one's ever got round to it. But, when I was appointed, the Group Accountant asked me to take it in hand."

I wonder why Jim hasn't mentioned this to me, or apparently, passed it on to anyone else? I think we ought to confront Chris about why she hasn't involved Malcolm or me in its implementation.

"Well, I wanted to surprise you. I often find that new information makes a bigger impact if I can produce a sample report out of the blue. It helps to illustrate the new insights. But I didn't imagine that I wouldn't have a chance to explain before you showed it to Malcolm."

She has a point. I decide to help her deal with Malcolm's defensiveness and ask her to explain the report's purpose.

"Well, you told me soon after I came that you wondered how much money we really make out of people like Kwikmart and Fareprice because of all the hassle, the management time and the special price concessions we give. Actually, Malcolm, you made a similar point when we were discussing selling costs a few weeks ago and you mentioned the time you spend dealing with some of the big accounts."

She seems more relaxed now, leaning back in the chair, sharing the eye contact between us and putting her ideas over in her usual confident way.

"Well, the idea of customer profitability analysis is that, every now and again, no more frequently than six months or even twelve, you do an analysis of sales, discounts, and long-term costs in order to highlight strategic issues."

"Now just what does that mean?" says Malcolm, quite aggressively. "What strategic issues are there? They're our third biggest customer, we need them and can't afford to lose them. Yet your report is suggesting we get rid of them."

"It isn't," says Chris, flushing.

"Now, hang on a minute, Malcolm. I don't think Chris is necessarily suggesting that."

"No, I'm not. That isn't a decision which a financial report could or should suggest. That would be a strategic decision and all I could do would be to evaluate the financial effects if you planned to do it. As I did for the catering contract if you remember."

"By taking avoidable costs you mean?" I say. She nods, looking pleased. She's noticed how I've understood that concept and raised it in the right context. It makes me feel confident enough to challenge her about the apparent inconsistency between avoidable costs and the apportionments in the customer profitability statement.

"All right, then," I carry on, "why therefore do you put all these cost apportionments in? It goes against what you said to the board about product profitability some while ago and also against your approach to the catering contract."

"But this is why I wanted to explain it to you, Phil. This is long-term strategic management information – to give you insights into your long-term cost structure. You use this to think about possible strategic options which can then be evaluated more precisely. The product profitability analysis was basically for looking at short-term product mix decisions, so the long-term cost structure wasn't important. The catering contract was the precise evaluation of the effects of a particular option. You see, management accounting is like a set of tools. You use different approaches for different purposes."

Malcolm still looks unhappy. The suggestion that Fareprice, one of his pet accounts and one which he brought in, are causing us to lose money, has obviously raised his hackles.

"But what purposes?" he demands. "You've accepted that we can't stop doing business with them so it's all theory – the sort of stuff you get in business schools."

I wonder if Malcolm knows of Chris's plans to go to Harvard? Chris looks concerned but is undeterred.

"I can't make you use the information, Malcolm. I accept

that the idea has been introduced to you very badly and I'm sorry about that. But at companies where they've used it – the whole of Universal's Detergents Division for instance – the sales and national accounts people have found many benefits."

"Name one," says Malcolm. "Closing down their top five accounts, I suppose."

"No. That's never been the outcome, but there have been cases where the discount structure has been re-examined. In one company where I implemented the system – in Universal's Pharmaceuticals Division – they found that the discounts were far different from what they expected and not always related to profit or volume. And under their previous system the discounts were not recorded systematically. All the invoicing was done on net sales after discounts."

Malcolm looks at me and I raise my eyebrows with a look that's meant to say "It's the same here, you know." He understands that I want him to take a more co-operative line. We both listen more intently and more positively to what she has to say.

For half an hour we hear more about the benefits and it broadens into a general discussion about the positive ways we might use the system. We talk about how the product mix of each customer influences the profitability of its business and how it is possible to change it to make more profit. Chris says that, in other Universal companies, this was the area where profit could most easily be improved without upsetting the customers.

We also discuss the possibility of negotiating potential trade-offs between price and operating costs, maybe giving a price concession in return for savings on interest or distribution costs.

Some Universal companies have apparently claimed considerable savings in costs as a result of changes in methods of operation which arose from using the statements. Chris admits that she has used fairly arbitrary methods to allocate the customer direct costs – cost per delivery for distribution, cost per order for administration and cost per salesman's call for selling. She agrees that, before we consider any cost reductions, we shall need to examine which ones can be made avoidable. Malcolm was fascinated to find that, each time a salesman calls, the average cost is nearly £100, and he says he might let his regional managers know this figure. Apparently the general indirect costs, all those which cannot be directly related to a customer's operations, are apportioned on a sales volume basis, and Chris concedes that this rather arbitrary final stage can be left out. But she says with a smile that showing a profit or loss, rather than a contribution, can draw people's attention to the figures. Malcolm says he knows what she means and we all laugh.

Chris tells us that, with most companies that have used the system, the biggest overall benefit felt by the sales people was just being well prepared before their negotiations with their larger clients. They'd done their homework and gone through the costs and they were more professional and more confident when dealing with the sophisticated buyers of these customers. They also knew where they should focus their attention from a long-term point of view and the areas where trade-offs and concessions could best be targeted. They all felt that this document was an essential guide before the annual price negotiations or before any important issue was discussed. Apparently most companies do it every six months and a few yearly, with ad hoc special reports when required. Most only do it for the top 10 per cent of clients, which usually accounts for well over 60 per cent of volume anyway.

She wins us over. Malcolm and I end up convinced that, used in the right way, these reports will help us concentrate on the important long-term issues with our bigger clients. We decide that the reports should not be circulated widely but should only go to management who deal with the customers concerned and it should be stressed that they are in no sense critical or competitive. Their production should be followed by a meeting about the client between the managers involved. The meeting should prepare the person who is to negotiate to develop the right approach and select the right issues.

I can tell that Chris is pleased as we get up and Malcolm prepares to leave my office. She's used her persuasive skills to good advantage again. As Malcolm is going she asks if she can have a further five minutes.

After Malcolm's gone, she looks at me and says, "Thanks".
"For what?"
"For helping me just then and for not holding my mood this morning against me."
"Forget it, Chris," I say as non-committally as I can. "You won the argument on its merits. You had a good case. That's why I was swayed and so was Malcolm."
"Can I give you something else while I'm winning?"
"Of course."
"I've produced the previous two months' key data sheet figures so you can compare it over the last three months. I'm also loading the graphs on the computer so you can see the trends. You have a look at the reports over the next few days and we can meet again to refine it. That's how good MI develops."
She leaves my office apparently very happy with life. As she opens the door she says: "By the way, it's my Harvard interview tomorrow. They're holding them in London so I won't be in until the afternoon. Had you remembered?"
I hadn't but I pretend I had. I wish her luck but don't really mean it. For business and personal reasons, I would love her to fluff it. But, in my heart, I know she won't. She's far too high calibre to be turned down, even by Harvard.
After she's gone, I look at the last two months' key data sheets. I study all the sections – production yields, labour efficiencies, shortages, labour turnover and absenteeism, sales volume and the financial details. I've seen most of them before but never together on one piece of paper. I get engrossed in them and, after half an hour, my action pad contains questions for every one of the management team. I can raise all these points at the next management meeting. And I think I'll invite Chris along, even if Berisford and Marshall are there. Too bad if I hurt their feelings; she's worth two of them and more.
She's right about the key data sheet. It does promote the sort of questions an MD ought to be asking but which can get lost amid all the data in our regular reporting system. Focusing on the key success variables is the secret. I jump as the phone rings.

Sylvia says, "Mr Moorley, Mrs Moorley just rang from the Trattoria. She couldn't hang on because she was in a call box. She said you promised to meet her at 12.30."

I look at my watch and my heart sinks. I'd lost track of the time and it's one o'clock. I'd arranged to meet Jean to discuss what the kids had said to me. How could I have forgotten? Damn, damn, damn. This job is so involving that I forget everything else. I don't deserve to have my family back. I say to Sylvia: "Ring the restaurant and tell her I'll be there in five minutes."

I rush out of my office hoping desperately that she'll still be there.

Chapter 16

I drive the one mile to the restaurant in reckless style. There's nowhere to park and I curse to myself as I try to find a place. In the end I leave the car on a yellow line and run the last few metres to the restaurant. Jean is just coming out looking angry.

"I'm sorry, Jean, I just got tied up in a meeting." I should have thought up a better excuse but it's too late.

"You never change, do you?" she says. "I thought this was one meeting you could have put before your work. You can forget lunch and you can forget any ideas of our getting together again."

She walks off briskly down the street and I follow rather pathetically, trying to talk to her as she goes. She looks straight ahead, ignoring my pleas to think again. I wonder how I must look to the many passers-by – it's a busy street and there are lots of lunchtime office workers around.

"When will I see you?" I say. "What about this weekend with the children?"

She turns to face me. "You can have the children on Sunday. And you can explain to them what's happened. I'm not going to tell them. And will you please stop following me."

It's hopeless to try and plead with her any more. Once she's in this kind of mood I've never been able to move her. And who can blame her? There's no excuse. It wasn't even the meeting with Malcolm and Chris that made me

173

late. It was looking at the new MI sheet. I hadn't put my meeting with Jean in Sylvia's diary and I suppose I'm just not used to fitting family events into my working day. But, whatever the reason, I've blown it and what will the children say when I meet them at the weekend? The idea of picking them up and taking them out again seems so depressing after the last two happy weekends with all of us together. But that's right out of the question now, at least for a while.

I find a parking ticket on the car. That's all I need. On the way back to the office, feeling tired and depressed, I remember that Prior is coming to see me for his weekly meeting this afternoon. I don't feel much like lunch so I call in at the shop next to the factory and buy some crisps and a chocolate bar. In my office I decide to tackle my in-tray, but without much enthusiasm. At the top is a pink envelope, the sort that Universal use to send out confidential memos. It's from Personnel Division. The memo, says:

General Managers' Workshop

Please note that you have been selected to attend this workshop for existing and potential company General Managers. It will take place on January 23rd–25th at the Metropole Hotel (details enclosed). Please note the pre-course work required in the enclosed briefing notes. As a central feature of the workshop will be presentation and discussion of Universal's published accounts, please ensure that you bring your copy with you.

JOHN WHITEHEAD
Personnel Director

The fact that the memo is signed by Whitehead emphasizes its status and importance. This must be a sign that I'm in line for Jim's or some other MD's job. It helps a little to lift my depression. I look at the papers inside to see if I know anyone on the course members list. Richard Watts is one. He's an American, brought over here to turn round one of Universal's meat companies. We met on another course a little while ago and got on well. Then another name makes me wince. Martyn Ames! How can he be coming, I wonder? Then I see that the course is the week before he's due to start with us. He must be coming over a week earlier to take in the course. Somehow having Ames on the list detracts from the pleasure I feel at being selected, but it's still a sign that things are going well for me at Universal. I wonder if Prior put my name forward?

The programme includes a presentation by the Chairman on company strategy, a session on the Universal accounts by the Financial Director and several other inputs by company and outside speakers. There's also group work on "Company Performance Measurement" followed by presentations and discussion. I wonder what that's about? I'll look at the briefing notes later.

During my meeting with Prior, I ask him about the workshop. He confirms that he nominated me but says I mustn't assume anything from it.

"I know," I say, "particularly as Martyn Ames is on it too."

"Is he?" says Prior. "I didn't know that. He must have been nominated by his previous MD. Still, you're both very eligible for it – it's for existing and potential GMs and you both have that potential, I'm sure. But Jim's still MD, Phil. You mustn't forget that. How is he, by the way?"

I feel very guilty about my visits to Jim. I've only been twice. I just haven't had the time recently with family and work commitments. Or was it that I just didn't want to go? On both occasions Jim seemed very weak and quite uninterested in what was happening at Lawrensons, so it was difficult to keep the conversation going. All he seemed to want to know was how I was treating Sylvia. I left my second visit convinced that he'll never come back as MD. But I'd better not to say this to Prior – it might be misunderstood.

"He's progressing, but still very weak," I say. "The doctors say he's healing physically but the shock is still affecting his progress. They reckon April or May at the earliest before he's back."

Before Prior goes I show him my MI sheet and the customer profitability statement. He seems impressed by the MI sheet and asks for a copy – he says he may ask for something similar for all the divisions he controls. "Always bogged down with too much bloody paper," he says.

He's obviously seen customer profitability statements before and says he's pleased we're looking at our main clients that way.

"You seem to be making strides with your management accounting, Phil. Who heads your finance function? I've forgotten."

"We don't really have anyone who heads it. Berisford was Company Secretary before the acquisition and he's now called Chief Accountant, but he's really only a book-keeper. We've also got Mike Marshall, the Cost Accountant. But this work has been done by Chris Goodhart, who came from Group a few months ago."

"Of course. An attractive girl if I remember and quite bright, so I've been told. You've been getting on well with her, have you, Phil?"

He raises his eyebrows significantly. I say nothing and smile, trying not to show my disapproval of his innuendo. Yet I know that if it had been any other female, I'd have been joining in the joke without any hesitation. Perhaps sensing my disapproval, he becomes serious again.

"If she's good, perhaps you should make her Chief Accountant and give Berisford some other title. I know the Group Accountants do all the cash management but you need someone to advise you on the financial aspects. And you shouldn't have three people doing financial jobs without someone having overall responsibility."

That could be a way of keeping her here, the top financial job and the chance of putting one over Marshall and Berisford. I'll talk to her about it when the time is right.

"I might just do that," I reply, still unable to use his Christian name. "Can I go ahead before Jim returns if I decide to?"

"You'll need to check with the Group Accountant, but I'm sure he won't object. They always like to see a Universal person at the top of the finance function."

I walk out with him, and after seeing him off, decide to go and talk to Chris in her office. Malcolm is in there with her and I see the familiar flipchart, which lists about a dozen big customers. As I come in, he's already getting up to go.

"We were just agreeing which customers we should produce customer profitability statements for," he says. I can almost hear Chris purring with contentment at having won him round so convincingly.

After he's gone, there's a silence while I think about the best way to raise Prior's suggestion. Then I remember her interview tomorrow. Harvard has been her main ambition and, though the Chief Accountant's job is a big one for someone of her age, she might feel that she'll never have another chance to go to Harvard. In any case I haven't yet cleared it with the Group Accountant. Best to leave it for the time being, to find the right time and place – she might turn Harvard down if it's put to her in the right way.

It occurs to me I'd better find a reason for coming in to see her.

"I've been nominated for a course," I say, "and I'm going to need your help." I tell her about the General Managers' Workshop and the financial content in particular.

"It will be a good excuse to show you some management ratios," she says. "I've been meaning to do that anyway. A lot of them could be useful for internal purposes, particularly the hierarchy of ratios."

"What's the hierarchy of ratios? Sounds frightening."

"Well, if you've got half an hour or so I'll show you." It will also be a good test of how far you remember our earlier sessions on the profit and loss account and balance sheet."

She delves in a drawer and pulls out two copies of Universal's annual report.

"Turn to page 23 and 24," she says.

I do so and see the Universal profit and loss account and balance sheet. Some of the words are a bit different from those we use internally but the principle is the same. They look like this:

Universal Products plc
Profit and loss account for 1987 (£m)

	1987	1986
Sales	15,271	14,003
Cost of sales	6,872	6,442
Gross profit	8,399	7,561
Other expenses	7,330	6,650
Trading profit	1,069	911
Interest payable	148	160
Profit before tax	921	751
Taxation	343	339
Earnings	578	412
Dividend	180	162
Retained profit	398	250

Universal Products plc
Balance Sheet – 1987 (£m)

Assets employed				
Fixed assets		3,561		2,984
Investments		627		420
Current assets				
Stock	2,092		1,969	
Debtors	2,719		2,298	
Cash	444		720	
		5,255		4,987
Total assets		9,443		8,391
Current liabilities (see note 16)		3,429		2,949
Total assets less CL		6,014		5,442
Long-term liabilities (see note 16)		1,723		1,449
Net worth		4,291		3,993
Represented by				
Share capital		430		430
Retained profits		3,861		3,563
Shareholders' equity		4,291		3,993

The profit and loss account seems fairly straightforward and very similar to our internal structure. I remember Chris told me before that earnings is another word for profit after tax and I ask her why they use that name.

"Earnings is just the American word for profit. But in this country it's used a lot by City analysts to describe profit after tax, what's left for the shareholders after everything – costs, interest and tax – has been covered. The Stock Exchange people tend to use their own buzz words."

"But it's not necessarily what's been paid to shareholders in cash," I say rather tentatively.

"No. That's the dividend. The directors have to decide what proportion of the earnings they can afford to pay in cash as dividend."

"Which depends on what they want to invest in future expansion, I suppose."

"That's right," she says, "so you need a cash flow forecast and agreed policies on capital expenditure and raising funds before you can decide on dividend. And then you need to balance this with what your shareholders need and expect."

"Which depends on what sort of shareholders they are?
"Absolutely. It sounds as if you know as much about this as I do. Yes, some shareholders want cash now. Others prefer the capital to be ploughed back for future growth. And that depends on their individual needs for cash and probably their personal tax positions too."

"What is Universal's dividend payment like compared to others?" I ask.

"Fairly well covered, actually," she replies, walking over to her flipchart. "This gives me a chance to show you the first ratio – dividend cover." She turns over the page of the flipchart and writes:

	1987	1986
Earnings	578	412
Dividend	180	162
Dividend cover	3.2	2.5

"Why don't you accountants speak the same language as other people?" I say. "I'd rather express dividend as a percentage of earnings. It would mean far more to me."

"I agree with you," she says, "but, as I said, the City have their conventions. I'll work out percentages if you like."

She does a few calculations and writes:

	1987	1986
Dividend as a percentage of earnings	31.1%	39.3%

"That seems mean to the shareholders," I say, "less than a third of profits being paid in cash. And look at the change from last year."

"You're right, Phil. Very interesting. I think it's the new capital expansion plans. They're going to need a lot of cash. And bear in mind that the shareholders still receive more in money terms and the share price is growing all the time."

We turn to the balance sheet and I try to recall what she told me about its meaning. Assets are on one side and on the other is a statement of where the money has come from to finance the assets. I ask Chris about two things that puzzle me – the phrase "represented by" and the fact that I can't see any loan capital on the balance sheet.

"It's the terminology and layout which the Companies Acts require. I don't like it personally but it's done for all published accounts in the EEC. "Represented by" is just the same as sources of finance really – I much prefer our phrase. It describes what that section of the balance sheet really means – where the money has come from to fund the net assets. The loan capital question is a bit more complex. Can you turn to note 16 on page 30?"

I do so and notice on the opposite page the Chairman's salary and how much the other Directors earn. They pay me peanuts by comparison. I also see all sorts of data about employees and the total wage bill. Note 16 says:

Note 16

Current liabilities	1987	1986
Trade creditors	2,482	1,776
Taxation owing	343	339
Other creditors	228	193
Bank overdraft	376	641
Total	3,429	2,949
Long-term liabilities		
6% debenture 1992/1997	500	500
Medium-term loans	1,223	949
	1,723	1,449

"You see," says Chris, "the loan capital's hidden away in the notes under long-term liabilities. I don't like this but it's just the way it's done for published accounts. The balance sheet I showed you in our earlier evening sessions had loan capital as a source of finance rather than as a liability which is deducted from assets. I think that's a better classification."

"What does 'debenture' mean?"

"A fixed interest, fixed repayment period loan. Taken out in the late 1960s and not repayable until 1992 at the earliest. Good for Universal but not much fun for those who put their money in."

I see what she means – I'm glad I didn't lend Universal money on that basis, the way inflation and interest rates have increased since, but it's cheap finance for the company.

"We'll go into loan capital some other time, Phil, but, before we leave this, could you note the overdraft? I'm going to use that in a moment so please remember it's in current liabilities."

"Why is it?"

"Because it's potentially subject to immediate recall. It could be required to be repaid at any time. Unlike the medium-term and long-term loans, which are due to be repaid at future dates, beyond this year."

She's now right into her teaching mode and obviously

enjoying it. My spirits begin to lift again after the lunchtime trauma, which I try to put out of my mind. I'm looking forward to analysing the Universal accounts and being able to understand them at last.

She writes up on another page of the flipchart:

THREE PRIMARY PERFORMANCE RATIOS

Then she draws three boxes:

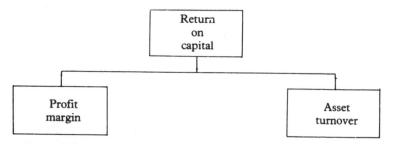

"OK, Phil, remember return on capital? How do you calculate it?"

This comes fairly easily because I've been using this ratio quite a lot in working on the budget and latest estimate figures.

"Trading profit to net assets employed," I reply.

"OK," she says, "try to extract the two figures from Universal's accounts."

The profit is easy – the trading profit of 1,069. The net assets must be the "total assets less current liabilities" figure because the heading of "net worth" is after taking off loan capital. We want to find the assets used by management to generate the trading profit.

"For 1987, 1,069 profits to 6,014 net assets," I say.

"Good," she replies, "but not quite right. The profit is right but the net assets need to be adjusted for the overdraft. At the moment we're including the overdraft in current liabilities, so I need to add it back to get the net assets involved in trading. Even though it's subject to short-term recall, the overdraft is really a source of funds to the business and should be excluded from current liabilities to calculate net assets."

"Like we excluded the negative cash balance when we calculated Lawrensons' budget capital employed?"

"Good. I'm pleased you remembered that. You're retaining this knowledge very well."

Her young attractive face makes me wistful. Should I forget my family, where I always seem to get it wrong, and gamble everything on this girl? No, the idea is ridiculous. She's not going to give up her career and her place at Harvard for a mixed-up middle-aged bloke like me. But maybe if I make her Chief Accountant, we'll work even closer together and eventually.

"Phil! Are you listening?" She's by the flipchart and she's written up underneath the boxes:

	1987	1986
Profit	1,069	911
Sales	15,271	14,003
Capital employed	6,390	6,083

"I've added back the overdraft of 376 and 641 to the total assets less current liabilities figures from the balance sheet. So we have net assets employed by management. OK?"

I nod and she continues.

"Now, I'm going to work out the three ratios of primary performance. You'll know two of them and the third is the link between them." She writes up:

		1987	1986
Profit margin =	$\dfrac{\text{Profit}}{\text{Sales}}$	$= \dfrac{1,069}{15,271} = 7.0\%$	$\dfrac{911}{14,003} = 6.5\%$
		X	X
Asset turnover	$= \dfrac{\text{Sales}}{\text{Cap. Emp.}}$	$= \dfrac{15,271}{6,390} = 2.39$	$\dfrac{14,003}{6,083} = 2.30$
		=	=
Return on capital	$= \dfrac{\text{Profit}}{\text{Cap. Emp.}}$	$= \dfrac{1,069}{6,390} = 16.7\%$	$\dfrac{911}{6,083} = 15.0\%$

"Now, Phil. What does that tell you?"

"Margins are up by 0.5 per cent. Must be a good trend. I've no idea whether 7 per cent is a good margin. Is it?"

"There's not really any such thing as a good or bad margin. It depends on your industry and your marketing policy. And, in any case, Universal are in so many businesses that it's difficult to work out what the average margin tells you. But, as you say, the trend is 0.5 per cent up on last year. That's a good sign. It's the link between margin and return on capital that's really important. It's a numerical but also a management relationship. Can you see it?"

I study the figures on the flipchart. Of course! $7 \times 2.39 = 16.7\%$. It must, because the sales entries cancel each other out if the first two equations are multiplied together. Even my school algebra covered multiplication of equations. But I still have problems understanding the middle ratio, asset turnover. That's not so easy to relate to as the other two. I ask Chris to explain it to me.

"It's a measure of volume," she says, "how much sales you generate in relation to assets employed. A combination of the quantity you sell and how good you are at controlling assets – fixed assets and stock for instance. Universal have increased this ratio to some extent in 1987. If it had gone down substantially, they could have achieved a lower return on capital despite the higher margin, see?"

I understand even more when she enters the figures in the three boxes. She explains that you can see the three ratios as a hierarchy, with return on capital at the top of the tree and the other two ratios cascading down from it:

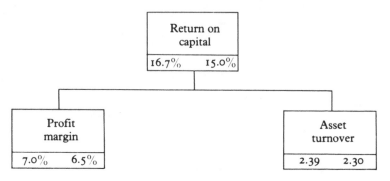

"This shows how ROC is a combination of profit margin and asset turnover – how managers generate profit margin from sales and then convert it into return on capital by generating sales from assets."

"Does the hierarchy go down any further?" I'm beginning to get quite interested in this concept. I can see it as a possible way of communicating messages to others in the organization about how they influence return on capital by their decisions.

She nods and draws on the flipchart:

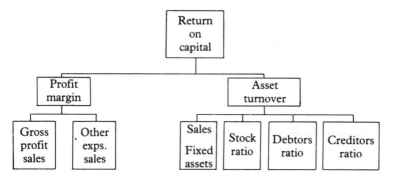

"Is that it?"

"Isn't it enough?" she replies, but with a smile, all the iciness of earlier forgotten. "You can go further and break down the costs into functional headings but we don't have the data on Universal's costs in the annual report. If you want to use this framework to analyse ratios in Lawrensons, we can break it down as much as we like. We could break costs and stocks down between departments, for instance."

"Can you work out some ratios for Lawrensons for me, using this framework? I think it would be useful to show some of our managers how their decisions affect the bottom line." Again I find myself using this familiar cliché. It seems so natural now that I don't even think twice and Chris hardly seems to notice.

"Yes. I'll do ratios for the budget and compare with this year and the year before if you like. The more years you include, the easier it is to spot the trends. Shall we work out Universal's ratios to complete the hierarchy? I'll just write up the other figures we need from the P and L and balance sheet."

She's filled up the sheet of paper so she sticks it up on the wall and writes on a clean sheet:

	1987	1986
Gross profit	8,399	7,561
Other expenses	7,330	6,650
Fixed assets	3,561	2,984
Stock	2,092	1,969
Debtors	2,719	2,298
Creditors	2,482	1,776

I can find all these figures except creditors in the profit and loss account and the balance sheet pages in the annual report.

"Remember note 16," says Chris. "Current liabilities were analysed. You'll see I've only taken trade creditors because the other creditors will be things like PAYE and other odds and sods. We only want credit taken from suppliers. Let me calculate these and we'll enter all the numbers in the hierarchy."

In a few minutes the numbers are on the flipchart:

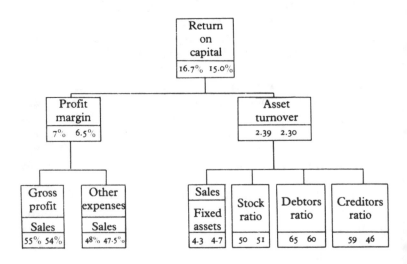

"Hmm. That's interesting," says Chris, "particularly the debtors and creditors changes. And the gross profit too. That's what ratios should do – pose questions. It might be worth looking a bit further in the accounts. But there's some nice points for you to raise on the course."

"Hang on, Chris. You're going too fast. Tell me where you've got these numbers from. I can see that the two on the left are percentages of sales. But what are the numbers on the right – percentages, ratios or what?"

"I'm sorry. I should have explained. The sales to fixed assets is a ratio, like the asset turnover. 15,271 divided by 3,561 gives you 4.3 for 1987. Notice how that's down, by the way. A sign that the extra investment in fixed assets is not yet producing the same volume as existing assets. This often happens soon after you've invested – it'll be one to watch in future years."

"What about the stock, creditors and debtors ratios?"

"They're expressed in days. Remember how we worked out Lawrensons' debtors ratio. Debtors divided by year's sales and converted to days by multiplying by 365. So for 1987 it's 2,719 divided by 15,271 times 365 – 65 days outstanding at the end of the year."

"Even more than Lawrensons!"

"Yes, though bear in mind that there's a lot of international divisions in Universal's figures and they often sell with longer credit periods than in the UK. What I'm curious about is that 5 days increase – all the pressure in the company has been to reduce working capital. Another good question for you to ask the Financial Director on the course. You see how ratios help you to ask questions?"

"Are the creditors and stocks in days too?" I ask.

"Yes. Just for convenience. It's the way I like to see them. Some people prefer to calculate them as a ratio of times turned over, particularly with stock. That could be expressed as 15,271 divided by 2,092, or just over 7 times turned over. It's only a question of how you prefer to think about it."

"The stock ratio is just about the same as last year," I point out, unjustifiably proud of this obvious statement, "but the creditors increase – 13 days – that's a hell of a big change. And 59 days is a lot of credit to take."

"That doesn't surprise me so much," says Chris. "There's been much more pressure to achieve return on capital employed this year and I suspect some company accountants have been taking extra credit at the end of the year, just to reduce capital employed. I agree it still seems a high figure of credit taken, though. In fact, it would be even more if you related it to purchases not sales. You still get a valid trend from year to year but, to be strictly correct, you should relate both stocks and creditors to cost-related figures. In both cases, the ratios would be higher if you worked them out on that basis."

I suddenly have an idea. It's probably a silly one but what the hell?

"Why don't you calculate the ratio of creditors to stock?" Chris looks at the flipchart and says, "I never have done. Why?"

"Because it tells you how much of your stock you've not paid for. Isn't that more relevant than relating it to sales?"

Gaining confidence, I walk to the flipchart, pick up Chris's calculator and turn over to a new sheet. I write up:

	1987		1986	
Creditors	2,482		1,776	
	-----	= 1.19	-----	= 0.90
Stock	2,092		1,969	

"If it's 1.0, it means you're financing all your stock by creditors," I say. "This way you relate creditors, based on purchases, to stock, valued at cost. It's more valid and more meaningful. Last year we weren't financing all our stock from creditors. This year we are and we're also financing 19 per cent of what we've already sold. That really is a significant change from 1986 to 1987."

"Phil," says Chris, "you've made it! I've never used that ratio but you're right. It's more valid and more useful. You're ready to take on the Chairman and the Financial Director on your course now. I always knew you had a flair for finance."

Looking at my watch, I'm surprised to find it's nearly 7 o'clock. I'm tired and feel I can't take any more figures but, after my depressing lunchtime experience with Jean, I don't feel like going home. Why not give it a try? But I must be very careful.

"Chris, you've said several times that we should be friends, real friends, and, just because we're the opposite sex, it shouldn't mean that we can't. Well, I've had a pretty rotten day until this last hour or so with you and I'd like someone to talk to this evening. Can I take you to dinner? As a friend, I promise."

I feel as if my whole future depends on her answer.

"Well, I was going to prepare for my interview," she says, "but I suppose I can do that later. But I mustn't be too late. And there are two other conditions."

"Name them."

"That we go somewhere well away from Lawrensons, you understand why. And that it genuinely is only as friends, good friends, I hope."

"Of course," I say, knowing perfectly well that this is the complete opposite of my real intentions. Some time, maybe not tonight, but some time, I'm going to convince her that we're much more than good friends.

Chapter 17

"But, Mr Moorley, is it not right that Lawrensons are a division of Universal International?" says the BBC interviewer, facing me across my desk with camera whirring and lights blazing.

"Indeed, that is true, and I can assure you that Universal insist that we take the socially responsible view. So, although we don't know the cause of the problem for certain, we have taken all our pork pies off the market for the time being."

"But aren't Universal going to be pressing you for short-term profit?"

"On the contrary, one of the benefits of being part of a big group is that we get support in situations like this and can afford to take the lowest-risk course of action."

"Mr Moorley, thank you very much."

The interviewer turns to the camera and makes a few final comments about the salmonella poisoning outbreak which has shattered our comfortable life at Lawrensons these last forty-eight hours. As the recording finishes, the interviewer, an attractive young woman in her mid-twenties, smiles and says "Well done." I'm amazed at the contrast with her aggressive attitude to me during the interview.

While the camera and the other equipment are being cleared away from my office, I wander outside and walk towards the despatch loading bay, hands in pockets, deep in thought. How strange life can be. Five weeks have passed since my row with Jean and that first night out with Chris.

Christmas has come and gone. A miserable Christmas too. The children have been understandably distant since I messed everything up and Jean doesn't want to talk to me at all. In the end I went to spend Christmas with my parents, who live in retirement in the Lake District. At least they were pleased to see me.

It wouldn't have been so bad if everything had been going well with Chris but one step just hasn't led to another. She really meant it when she said "good friends" and I don't know how to progress to the next stage. I've taken her to dinner twice more and enjoyed her company but, if I'm honest, I have to admit that the relationship is going nowhere. I've not yet offered her the Chief Accountant's job because the Group Accountant has only just come back with a clearance. I wonder how attractive the offer will seem compared to the glamour of the States? Apparently the Harvard interview went well and she should hear quite soon now.

And now this! At least everything at Lawrensons was fine. The year ended with profits well up on latest estimate, breaking the two million barrier with £2,050,000. Orders for next year were also well up and we could see real hope of moving the return on capital well over 10 per cent, even in the mid-teens. But one dodgy batch of pork pie filling can change all that. Fortunately no one has died, but a number are in hospital and it will take several days before we can get full permission from the Health Authority to restart production. And Heaven only knows how long it will be before customers feel it's safe to start buying again.

I see the BBC van driving out, the interviewer in the passenger seat.

"Goodbye, Mr Moorley," she says. "You did very well. All you people seem so well trained these days. I'll call you again it we need a follow up interview. This will be on the regional news this evening and it may even make the national bulletin. Bye."

I don't like to tell her that I've never had any training to appear on TV. I just said what Prior had told me to say when he rang earlier today. Still I feel it went well too, and this girl seems sincere. She waves as the van drives off.

I don't feel like going back to the office or doing any work at all. Something like this makes you so keyed up that it's impossible to concentrate on routine things. But the January wind is cold and the despatch loaders are beginning to wonder why I'm wandering around their yard. I go inside and make for Chris's office – she's always good to talk to and I haven't had a chance to discuss the food poisoning outbreak with her. I wonder how she'll reconcile it with Appleby's alleged efficiency – it's ironic that something like this should happen when Appleby has such an obsession with hygiene. All those years when Wilf was Production Director and it was all rather careless, nothing like this ever happened. Poor old Appleby's had the Group Technical Director down here like a shot and he's been with him ever since. I can't help feeling a sneaking pleasure that Appleby seems to be getting all the flak while I could be on the 6 o'clock news.

Chris smiles warmly as I enter her office. I wish I could manage the next step, to being more than friends, but I must hang on until the time is right.

"I didn't expect you'd make it," she says, "with all the drama. And you're a little early but I'm ready."

I look at her blankly.

"Our second session on the Universal accounts," she says. "You said you'd like to have another run through in the week before your course."

"I'm sorry, Chris, I'd completely forgotten. I don't even think I'll be going on the course now. I just wanted someone sane and sensible to talk to. Believe it or not I've just been interviewed for the BBC News."

I can't help feeling smug about this. Despite my middle age, my vanity is as strong as ever. I tell her all about the events of the last forty-eight hours, from the initial visit by the Health Inspector to the closing of the pie department and all the contact with the media. I dramatize my description to impress her, secretly hating myself for doing so. Once I've finished my story, she responds as only a born accountant could.

"We'll have to work again on the budget, won't we? Usually we only update quarterly in Universal but there'll be such an impact on pie volumes that we'll need a revised estimate. I'll start work on it tomorrow. And it's going to decimate this month's profits. I was looking forward to producing the January control information, but the variances will be all haywire now."

I sit down opposite her desk and think about this evening. The empty flat is not at all appealing and I'd like to be with someone after all the trauma of today. I'll run through the Universal accounts with Chris and then, all being well, take her out for a meal.,

"Penny for your thoughts," she says.

"I'm thinking that I'll have a look at the Universal accounts after all," I say, "as long as you'll come for a meal with me afterwards."

"On one condition."

"I thought it was always on that condition." I smile with a mixture of resignation and hope.

"No. I don't mean that. My new condition is that I pay. I can't let you buy me meals for ever despite your salary being more than mine."

"It's a deal," I say, showing more enthusiasm than I feel. Everything she does and says seems to emphasize how much she intends to keep me at arm's length.

"OK," she says, "Let's go through the Universal accounts again. Do you need me to go over the ratios we looked at last time or can you remember those?"

"No need, Chris, I've remembered them and I've been meaning to tell you that I've actually used them. I calculated the three primary performance ratios and some of your hierarchy for Kwikmart and Fareprice from their published accounts. I spent all last Sunday morning on it, believe it or not."

"And did it help? I seem to remember once telling you that you could benefit a lot from looking at customers' financial results."

"All right. No need to rub it in," I smile, "you were right. Combined with the customer profitability statement, it's a very powerful way of sorting out the important issues. And Malcolm was quite surprised on Monday when I came in with a lot of points for him to use in his negotiations."

"Which ratios were most useful?"

"Profit margin. Return on capital. I was interested how Kwikmart had a lower margin than Fareprice but still made a higher return on capital because of their higher asset turnover. I think it's mainly to do with product mix. I was also surprised at the differences in the stock and creditor ratios – Fareprice seem to take much more credit from us than their average ratio shows. Malcolm's going to bring up payment period when we discuss terms for this year."

"There's no doubt about it, Phil. You've broken through your mental block about finance. You're no longer dependent on me. You're actually doing your own analysis, which is a big step forward. Can I tackle some more advanced issues?"

"I wouldn't bank on it. Don't get carried away." But I'm more than pleased at what she's said, particularly because I know it's true. I'm now seeing how figures relate to management decisions and I'm developing the confidence to dig deeper and analyse further.

"OK," she says, walking towards the flipchart, "I've got copies of the Universal accounts. Let's have a look at the profit and loss account and balance sheet again."

She gives me the report and I turn to pages 23 and 24, the familiar profit and loss account and balance sheet.

Universal Products plc
Profit and loss account for 1987 (£m)

	1987	1986
Sales	15,271	14,003
Cost of sales	6,872	6,442
Gross profit	8,399	7,561
Other expenses	7,330	6,650
Trading profit	1,069	911
Interest payable	148	160
Profit before tax	921	751
Taxation	343	339
Earnings	578	412
Dividend	180	162
Retained profit	398	250

Balance sheet for 1987

		1987		1986
Assets employed		3,561		2,984
Investments		627		420
Current assets				
Stock	2,092		1,969	
Debtors	2,719		2,298	
Cash	444		720	
		5,255		4,987
Total assets		9,443		8,391
Current liabilities (see note 16)		3,429		2,949
Total assets less CL		6,014		5,442
Long-term liabilities (see note 16)		1,723		1,449
Net worth		4,291		3,993
Represented by				
Share capital		430		430
Retained profits		3,861		3,563
Shareholders' equity		4,291		3,993

"Now. Last time we concentrated on profitability at the operational level. We studied profit margin and ROC – how good the management are in the market place. We took trading profit because that's what operating management influence. Right?"

I nod and she carries on.

"Well, there's another way of approaching profitability and that's from the shareholder point of view. As an investor – what do I get out from what I put in? They're going to be interested in profit after tax because that's what's left for them, either to be paid as dividend or to be ploughed back. So how would you work out a profitability ratio which measures the efficiency of the management from a shareholder point of view?"

"Earnings of 578," I say and she nods encouragingly. On the balance sheet I see the share capital figure, "on share capital invested of 430."

"That would be a fantastic return, Phil. Over 100 per cent. No, the share capital's a historic figure showing how much actual capital has been put in since the company was first formed. But Universal has mainly been funded by retained profits over the years and that's just as much part of the shareholders' investment as the share capital. It's their money which they've allowed the Directors to keep in the business."

"How about the total shareholders equity – share capital and retained profits?"

"Good," she says and writes up:

	1987	1986
Earnings	578	412
Shareholders' equity	4,291	3,993
Return on equity	13.5%	10.3%

"So it's a measure of the real bottom line return which the shareholders are getting," I say. "Presumably you can compare this with other types of investment or with the return from investing in other companies?"

"Yes," says Chris, "though there is the other factor of share price growth which isn't taken into account in this measure. This is more of a management ratio. But management in the total sense, not operational performance but tax management and gearing too."

"Now you've lost me. I can see how the ability to manage tax affects that ratio, but not gearing. I thought gearing was to do with borrowing levels, not shareholder return."

"It is to do with borrowing levels, but gearing is also an important factor in determining return on equity. Let me show you."

She turns to a new page of the flipchart and writes up:

Assets	Profit
200	40

"Now," she says, "this is your company. Making 20 per cent ROC. We'll forget about tax for simplicity."

Despite my traumatic day, I'm still managing to concentrate and have become quite interested. I've often heard Prior going on about Universal's gearing and I've always wondered why it's so important.

"You have the choice of funding your company two ways: nil gearing or 1 to 1."

She writes up:

Option 1 Shareholders' equity 200

Option 2 Shareholders' equity 100
Loan capital 100
Total sources 200

"Is that what option 2 is called," I ask, "1 to 1 gearing? I thought you called it 50 per cent before."

"Yes. Remember I told you that there were different ways of expressing it. Some people call it 1 to 1 debt/equity ratio. Some would call it 100 per cent. Just to be different, other analysts call it 50 per cent because the 100 loan capital is 50 per cent of the total. I know it's confusing but people do use different labels. The meaning is the same however you express it."

"Is that level high?"

"It's getting towards being high, but a lot depends on the profit levels, the industry you're in and the economic climate in which you're operating. Often the level of 1 to 1 is thought to be a bit of a watershed. There's as much coming from loans as there is from shareholders. Now, which way of financing your business would you prefer? Option 1 or option 2, assuming, say, interest rates of 13 per cent? Why don't you come and work out the return on equity in each case?"

She hands me the felt pen and I go to the flipchart. I write up under Option 1:

Shareholders' equity 200 Profit 40

Return on equity 20%

"Good," she says, "there is nil gearing so the return on capital is the same as the return on equity. It all goes to the shareholders. Now try Option 2."

I write up:

Shareholders' equity	100	Profit before interest	40
Loan capital	100	Interest	13
Total sources	200	Profit	27
Return on equity	27%		

"So," she says, "you see why gearing is important to return on equity. As long as you're profitable and your return exceeds the interest rates, high gearing will give you a better return on equity. There's less shareholder investment but they make a higher return because they pick up the premium of profit over the interest rate."

"So high gearing is a good thing?" I always thought it was the other way round.

"It's good news, bad news. You make a higher return but you increase your risk by doing so. The more you borrow, the more you commit yourself to fixed interest, which is OK as long as profits are still exceeding the interest rate. But as soon as that changes, high gearing can be the factor that leads you into bankruptcy. That's why the banks look at the gearing ratio very carefully. They're the ones who'll be worried if it's more than 1 to 1."

Keen to demonstrate my increasing knowledge, I feel enough confidence to challenge the bankers' approach.

"That seems very arbitrary because surely it all depends on the business and its profit levels, as you've just said. And presumably some borrowing can be very cheap. Remember you told me about Universal's debentures with low fixed interest. Surely it's the ratio of interest cost to profit that's more important."

"You're dead right, Phil. I think I'll give up these sessions. You're beginning to teach me now. There is a ratio which I forgot to mention. Interest cover. Trading profit to interest payable. Rather like working out how your net salary relates to your mortgage payment to assess gearing in your personal life. Now let's work out Universal's ratios on both these bases."

While she's working these out, I think more about this

analogy to your personal life. Yes, I'm highly geared, big mortgages on two properties since I bought my flat. Loan for Jean's car. Yet this has been less of a problem since I took over as acting MD and received a £10,000 p.a. temporary increase. Yes, it's income or profit which is the key to whether you can afford to be highly geared.

She's written up:

	1987		1986
Shareholders' equity		4,291	3,993
Loan capital	1,723		1,449
Overdraft	376		641
Total borrowing		2,099	2,090
Debt to equity		0.49	0.52

"You notice I've included the overdraft," she says, "because even though it's in current liabilities, it still bears interest and has the same risk. Remember we found this information from short- and long-term liabilities in the notes last time."

"So it's down from last year," I say, "and it means that total borrowing is now less than half of shareholders' funds. I wish you'd express it in percentages."

"Yes, you can if you like. The only problem is, as I said before, that some do it as a percentage of shareholders' equity, some as a percentage of the total."

"I prefer my ratio – the interest to profit one. Can you write that one up?"

	1987	1986
Trading profit	1,069	911
Interest	$\dfrac{1{,}069}{148} = 7.2$	$\dfrac{911}{160} = 5.7$

"You've got it the wrong way round again," I say. "Surely it's better to do it as a percentage. That's how I'd like to think of it in my personal life. What percentage of your salary goes to pay the mortgage?"

The phone rings and, as I'm nearest, I pick it up. It's Sylvia.

"Mr Moorley," she says, disapproval in her voice, "we've been looking everywhere for you. I wanted to remind you that it's nearly six o'clock. The lady from the BBC told me you'd probably be on the news. Mr Davies has the television on in his office."

I know very well how often the BBC say they'll show things and then they don't. And I'm interested in what Chris is saying and enjoy being with her. I can't be bothered to trek all the way over to Malcolm's office.

"Ask Malcolm to record it, Sylvia. We'll see it later. I'll probably be here for another half-hour or so. Sorry I didn't tell you where I'd gone."

"We'll go up later and see the tape if you like," I say to Chris after I've put the phone down. "Not of course that I'm really interested in seeing myself."

She laughs with me. Over the last few weeks we've begun to laugh together much more. We share a similar sense of humour and have found ourselves giggling about people and situations at Lawrensons when we've eaten out together.

"OK, teacher," I say. "What now?"

"There's only one other financial dimension and that's liquidity. It's not really as important as gearing but the banks look at it very carefully and you ought to know the usual ratios."

"Liquidity presumably concerns the cash in the balance sheet, does it?"

"Not just the cash. It's all current assets, stock, debtors and cash. It measures whether you have enough current assets to pay off your current liabilities if required. It may never happen but the liquidity ratios measure how you would be placed if it did. Again it's the banks who are most interested and like to see liquidity high. From a management performance point of view, it's better in some ways to have low liquidity."

I wonder what she means by this?

She writes:

Liquidity ratio	1987	1986
Current assets	5,255	4,987
Current liabilities	——— = 1.53 3,429	——— = 1.69 2,949

"I see it's gone down a bit. Why's that?"

"I think it's the cash position," Chris replies. "Cash has gone down and the overdraft's gone up. And remember the increased creditors ratio we looked at last time. That will push up current liabilities and bring the current ratio down."

"What's the current ratio?"

"Sorry. Just another name for the liquidity ratio. I'm confusing you with terminology again. It's the same with the next measure – it can be called the acid test or the quick ratio. Let me show you."

Acid test ratio	1987	1986
Current assets (less stock)	3,163	3,018
Current liabilities	——— = 0.92 3,429	——— = 1.02 2,949

"This ratio excludes stock and thus takes cash and debtors only. That's because stock is more difficult to convert into cash quickly than the others and its valuation may be questionable if you have to realize it in an emergency. Again you can see it's gone down, for the same reason as the liquidity ratio."

"But I'm still not quite sure what they tell you. Is there a norm?"

"The banks like to see two for the liquidity ratio and one for the acid test, but it's very dependent on industry and reputation. It's assessing how far you could cover your short-term liabilities if your creditors wanted paying and the bank called in the overdraft. It may never happen and many businesses exist permanently with low liquidity because their track record enables them to maintain confidence. With reputable companies, it's only the trend that's interesting. The fact that the acid test is below one isn't going to cause anyone to lose confidence in Universal."

"Why did you say that low liquidity can indicate good management performance?"

"Well, think of capital employed. Low liquidity means low working capital. Take retailing, for instance. You'll find that the Kwikmarts of this world will have very low liquidity – almost certainly below one – because they have low stocks, no debtors and they don't leave cash lying around. But they do take credit from people like us. So the more efficient a retailer is, the lower his liquidity will be."

"In other words, a lot depends on the industry."

"Absolutely. But it still means that a retailer could very quickly go bust if confidence is lost. That's why it's nice to see low gearing if you're in retailing. Liquidity's not so much of a problem if there is plenty of borrowing capacity. The worst possible situation is poor liquidity and high gearing. That's a combination the bankers are most concerned about. But poor liquidity on its own need not be a problem if the business is successful."

Again the phone rings and this time Chris answers it. She jerks back in her chair, puts her hand over the receiver and whispers, "Phil, it's the Chairman. Sir James wants to speak to you."

It's not often these days that I get butterflies in my stomach, but the thought of speaking to Sir James really brings them on. In Universal the Chairman is regarded as GOD and rarely speaks directly to anyone working for one of the companies. Every few years there might be a ritual visit, but we've never seen Sir James at Lawrensons in the five years he's been Chairman.

"You'd better put him on," I say, trying to calm down but already I feel my hand shaking. I take up the receiver and say hello.

"Sir James Mosely to speak to you, Mr Moorley," says a crisp male voice on the line.

While I'm waiting, Chris whispers, "Do you want me to go?" and I shake my head. "Good luck," she says and I know she means it.

I wonder if he's going to lay into me about the salmonella poisoning? It must be something to do with that. Does Prior know the Chairman's ringing me?

"Hello, Moorley," booms Sir James, "sorry to hear about your problem out there. Prior's kept me fully informed and I know the technical people are doing all they can. But I'm ringing to congratulate you on your television interview. Particularly as Prior tells me you're only standing in as MD and you've had no training. But you were most impressive. Particularly the way you mentioned Universal's social responsibility."

"Er – thank you," – what do I call him? – "Sir James," I say, "it's good of you to ring."

"Not at all, Moorley. Prior tells me you're on the course next week so I look forward to meeting you then. Goodbye."

I put the phone down and sink back into my chair. Praise from the Chairman! Now I'll have to go on the course. Eat your heart out, Martyn Ames! I must get Jim's job now.

"Why did he ring, Phil," asks Chris.

"To congratulate me on my BBC news appearance. You're talking to a TV star. We'd better go up and see the video. Then we can have dinner."

"Just before we go, Phil, there's something I want to tell you. I've been meaning to all afternoon but I haven't had the chance. I've just heard from Harvard and I've got my place."

Every time something good happens in my career, something bad seems to happen in my private life. My euphoria turns to gloom, but I still have a card to play.

"Congratulations, Chris," I say, "We'll have some champagne over dinner. And I'm going to put a proposition to you. No, not the kind of proposition you're thinking about. I want to offer you a job, a bigger job, here at Lawrensons."

She looks at me in surprise.

"Tell me more," she says.

"Over dinner. Let's go and see my star performance first."

Chapter 18

I'm sitting in a hotel bedroom, converted into a course syndicate room, with five other "existing or potential General Managers" of Universal. One of them is Richard Watts, the American I knew from a previous course, and we exchange knowing looks as one of our group tries to dominate the discussion. We're in syndicates preparing questions about the Universal accounts for a discussion with the Financial Director. This is the afternoon of the first day of the course and we've just gratefully escaped into groups after a morning of crashing boredom – the Chairman's description of our future strategy.

I met the Chairman at yesterday evening's sherry party – standing in an awkward circle, as Sir James made his own brand of small talk. To my chagrin, he didn't even remember my name when I introduced myself – his memory is notoriously short. I got away as soon as possible and went to bed to read the book about divisional performance measuring which Chris had recommended to me. Tomorrow's session is about that and I've been reading it up so I can make my contribution to the debate.

I should be concentrating on the group discussion but as our verbose, self-appointed chairman sounds off about profit margins, my thoughts drift back to my evening with Chris just over a week ago when I told her she could be Chief Accountant of Lawrensons. She seemed very interested but asked to delay her decision until my return at the end

end of the week. I was flattered when she said she would like to be certain I was going to be Managing Director on a permanent basis, but we both realize that this decision would not be in time.

"But it's not just the profit margin," says Richard Watts and I prick up my ears. "We should be asking about the change in return on capital."

"Which is the most important?" asks one of the other group members, a pleasant chap with a broad Yorkshire accent who seems to have even less financial knowledge than I had a few months ago.

"I think it's profit margin," says the verbose individual, "how much of each sale we make in profit."

"No," says Richard, "it's ROC. That's the name of the game in Universal. How good we are at generating profit from assets."

I decide to join in. "I don't think that it need be either/or. They can be linked together by a third ratio, the asset turnover. Let me show you."

I walk over to the flipchart in the corner and sketch out the hierarchy of ratios which Chris showed me. Within fifteen minutes we've got all the performance and working capital ratios in the hierarchy, just as Chris and I did that evening when I first took her out to dinner.

The rest of the group look on with interest and even the Yorkshireman seems to understand. Our self-appointed group chairman keeps quiet and nods passively while Richard Watts's expression seems to say – "whatever's happened to you these days?"

I'm nominated to give a presentation on behalf of our group and pose the various questions which arise from the comparisons of '86 and '87 ratios within the hierarchy. One member draws a neat transparency for the overhead projector and finishes it just in time for us to go back to the lecture room.

I enjoy making the presentation, my newfound confidence in financial matters giving me great pleasure. There's even a ripple of applause from the course when I finish and the Financial Director makes some appreciative comments which sound sincere. He also answers the questions which our presentation raises, which reminds me how ratios can be so powerful in the way that they raise issues for discussion.

After the session we adjourn to the bar and I chat to Richard about life in Universal. I tell him about what happened to Jim and my present situation, quietly because Martyn Ames is standing quite close by. I've only managed to say a quick "hello" to Ames since the course started. I must have a chat with him some time during the course.

He comes over to Richard and me in the bar and offers to buy us a drink. Despite his friendly manner I still can't help resenting his good looks and his over-confident air.

"Congratulations on your presentation," he says. "Everyone was most impressed. I didn't know you had a financial background."

"I don't. I've just had to educate myself to cope with all the bean counters at Universal."

"Like your young lady management accountant? She didn't seem much like a bean counter to me."

"No, she's not. In fact she's the one who's helped me get to grips with the financial matters. I'd have found it much more difficult to cope with the MD's job without her help."

"Well, I'm looking forward to joining you next week," he says. "Maybe I can help too. You know I was once a bean counter myself."

We laugh and then chat on for a while. Ames is going out of his way to be helpful. I wonder if he senses I'm now the favourite for Jim's job? Everyone in Universal knows that some of the most promising careers have been ruined by failure to get on with one's boss on the way up.

After a while, Ames goes over to another group in the bar but, before he goes, we agree to meet over lunch the next day for me to brief him about Lawrensons in general and the salmonella outbreak in particular. Production is now restored and I'm getting daily reports on sales volume, which is still painfully slow to recover.

The rest of the course drifts into dinner but, as there are no formal sessions this evening, Richard suggests that we go to the local pub and then on to London for a meal. I wonder how it will be seen by the others, but I like Richard and agree to go with him. As we drive along, he tells me how he's hankering for a return to New York but Universal don't have any job vacancies in the States. He seems very opposed to Universal and their philosophies and I have the impression that he'd leave if the right job offer came along. He tells me some of his frustrations.

"It's the way they measure performance, Phil. I've worked myself into the ground to turn the meat company round and we're now getting a return on capital of about 15 per cent. But our Divisional Director isn't satisfied and produces a bloody league table showing me next to the bottom. He doesn't seem to understand that you can't compare a company like mine in the north of England with those in the south. And on top of that, the centre insist that we produce quite a lot of goods for other Universal companies and the transfer price just doesn't give us enough margin."

"I haven't seen any league table," I reply. "I'd be about the same as you. We're budgeting for about 10 per cent and that's unlikely now we've had this problem with pies."

"Well, you'll get a league table," says Richard. "All divisions are producing them, so I've been told. It's a new policy. And what irritates me is that at the top of our league is a tinpot little delicatessen producer who makes 35 per cent return but is about a tenth of my size. He'll just stay small and continue to be top of the table."

The book I was reading about divisional performance measurement discussed some of these problems and suggested some alternatives.

"Look, Richard," I say, "they're discussing the performance measurement system tomorrow on the course. Why don't we bring up some of these issues with the Financial Director and the other Universal people. The situation you describe is ridiculous – there's no reward for size and no motivation to grow. Tomorrow morning I'll show you a book I've been reading."

We agree to meet over breakfast and then we forget about Universal for a while as, together, we put the world to rights. It's good to relax with a friend. I've never had a male friend since I married Jean – we were so obsessed with each other that we never really had a need for friends except for a few families with children the same age as ours. Then, after the divorce, it was difficult to pick up old friends or find new ones.

Back in my hotel bedroom, I turn again to my book. It's by some American business school professor and it's surprisingly readable. I read the chapter on return on capital and I realize how complex the whole issue really is. Return on capital is fine as a measure of performance of the whole business, but there are all sorts of problems when you start to use it on companies or divisions within an integrated group. I make a few notes and work for an hour before tiredness sets in and I go to bed.

Next morning Richard and I find a table in a corner of the restaurant. He seems rather pessimistic about our chances of changing the way Universal does things.

"Now come on, Richard," I say, "we won't get a better chance than this. The course requires us to work in groups and prepare presentations about our views for the Financial Director. And the Chairman's coming again this afternoon so he could be sitting in too."

"OK. Let's see what you want to say."

"The first thing is that Universal don't seem to know whether they're assessing us as shareholders who want a return or as managers evaluating and controlling our performance. They take profit before tax, which highlights management performance, but then they produce that league table which implies that everyone should be getting the same return."

"How do you mean?" Richard's getting interested now.

"Well – to produce a simple league table of return on capital is failing to take into account the special factors applying to each business. Like your inter-company trading and your special problems in the north. They're behaving like a shareholder. It's valid to have league tables for strategic reasons but not to assess our performance."

"Strategic reasons?"

"Like whether to close companies down or to invest in similar operations. But you can't compare management performance with a league table, particularly when we're all in different businesses."

"You could have a league table based on relative performance against budget."

"Yes, you could, though you'd have to be sure that the
budgets were all equally realistic." I think back to my earlier
discussions with Jim and Prior about the effect of Universal's
political pressures on the realism of our budget levels.

We go on to talk about the problems of return on capital
as a measure. We talk more about the "stay small" problem,
the small division making a high return, top of the league
table but no incentive to expand.

"But you can't just take profit in money terms," says
Richard. "It has to be related to assets employed at some
point. I guess the real point is that there should be some
separate objective for growth."

"Too bloody right," I say, beginning to feel quite passion-
ate about the whole subject. I'm becoming more and more
aware that this is a management issue rather than a financial
one. "That's the whole point. Therefore there should be
not just one financial measure but a whole range of objectives.
It's the obsession with return on capital which is the real
problem. And there is a method of measurement which helps
to solve this problem of growth. Let me show you."

I don't tell Richard that this is straight out of the text
book. I write down on the breakfast menu these figures:

	Division A	Division B
Assets	1,000,000	300,000
Profit	150,000	75,000
Return on capital	15%	25%

"All right, Richard, your problem is that you think you're
better than B because you're bigger, but the performance
measure doesn't show it. So we need a measure which com-
bines both profitability and growth. Now, let's say that
Universal require 10 per cent to cover their cost of capital
and justify the risks of the business. You can then charge

this level to each division and measure performance on the
excess. Like this. . ."

I write:

	Division A	Division B
Assets	1,000,000	300,000
Profit	150,000	75,000
10% charge on assets	100,000	30,000
"Super Profit"	50,000	45,000

"Why super profit?" asks Richard.

"That's just my name for it. The book I've read calls
it residual income. But it represents your contribution over
the required return."

"And if I'm in division A, I'm above B in the league
table because I deliver more cash after covering the required
return."

"I thought you didn't believe in league tables. Most people
only believe in them when the system makes them top."

We laugh at this and then it's time for us to go to our
session. On the way, I ask Richard if he'll make the presentation with me, providing we can get the group to agree.

"You do it, Phil. Between you and me, I may not be
with Universal much longer, so you make the presentation.
You've more to gain. But bear in mind it's a high risk. You're
on very sensitive ground."

The morning is another painfully boring one. The Director
of Management Services describes Universal's computer
strategy and the Personnel Director talks about management
development policies. He goes on about the need to provide
opportunities for young general managers, but my mind keeps
on wandering back to the issue of financial performance
measurement, which I'm seeing more clearly all the time.
As points occur to me, I make notes. There are one or two
other problems about profit measurement which confirm that

it shouldn't be such an obsession. There are the discretionary costs, like advertising and research, which you can cut to help profit this year. All the pressure in Universal is for a Managing Director to do just that, achieve a good return and then transfer to some other company leaving a long-term mess for someone else. The only way to stop this is to have objectives in these areas which are as important as profit in the assessment of performance.

I'm still absorbed in this when I notice everyone getting up for lunch. I join Martyn Ames in the bar, we find a corner and I brief him about Lawrensons. He's interested in what's happening and proves helpful and supportive. He's pleased to hear about my offer to Chris.

"You must have someone at the top of the finance function, Phil," he says. "It will help me because I don't want to be seen as a finance person. I want to support you as Deputy MD and be involved in general management issues."

"I'm not sure for how long though, Martyn," I say, warming to his support. "Jim's due back in April or May. Though, between you and me, I wonder if he'll come back at all. Then I imagine they'll have to choose between you and me."

"There's something you ought to know, Phil. I've asked not to be considered. I don't think I'm ready and neither do Personnel Division. The plan was for a year or so as Deputy, then maybe take over. So it's either you or they transfer in someone else. They could still do that, you know."

I'm pleased that Ames is no longer a contender, but his comment brings home how narrowly I've been seeing the whole situation. They could still bring in an experienced man to fill the vacuum until Ames or some other young Turk is ready.

As we leave for our briefing for the session on performance measurement, I say to Ames, "By the way, Martin, what do you think about Universal's performance measurement system?"

"Full of conflicts and paradoxes. They make you profit-accountable and then tie your hands behind your back because of all the central decisions. In Hong Kong our profit was dictated solely by the international transfer pricing system. They changed Head Office overheads around just to minimize tax. Then they tried to make our MD profit-accountable. Crazy."

We go to our seats and the Financial Director briefs us. He says, "I want you to analyse the strengths and weaknesses of our financial performance measurement system. We're in the process of reviewing the way we do it and we genuinely want your comments and recommendations."

We all troop off to our syndicates and the same group as yesterday gathers in our room. Before yesterday's chairman can speak, Richard says, "I'd like to suggest that Philip here takes the chair this time. I know he's done a special study of this subject so he can make sure we keep to the right issues."

The chairman of yesterday looks frustrated but doesn't know how to object. The Yorkshireman says, "I agree. Philip helped us a lot yesterday. Fire away."

I take the group through all the issues I've been talking and thinking about this last week. It broadens into a general discussion and we list the strengths and weaknesses on a flipchart.

STRENGTHS

- Return on capital easily understood.
- Focus on ROC creates a "bottom line" orientation.
- Gives managers financial accountability.

No one can think of any more strengths so we move on to the weaknesses:

WEAKNESSES

- Encourages companies to stay small.
- Can create obsessive concentration on profit at the expense of the long term.
- profit accountability can conflict with centralized decision making.
- Allocation of central overheads creates dissatisfaction.

This last point comes from the Yorkshireman, who feels strongly that his company's profit should not be reduced

the Financial Director and the Chairman show no response at all. I wonder if I'm making the biggest mistake of my life as I move on to the final flipchart which shows recommendations:

RECOMMENDATIONS

1 Only publish league tables which show relative performance against budget.
2 Ensure that central constraints and special circumstances are taken into account whenever performance is evaluated.
3 Measure companies on contribution before central costs rather than net profit.
4 Measure in money terms on "super profit" rather than as a percentage.
5 Ensure that profit is seen only as one of a number of key objectives for managing directors.
6 The board to ensure that all the individually negotiated performance levels reconcile with shareholders' objectives.

This last recommendation must seem very cheeky. I sense a chilly atmosphere as I round off the presentation – there's a silence as I walk back to my seat and I notice one or two course members looking round to see how the Chairman is reacting.

The Financial Director gets up. "Thank you Group 3," he says. "At last someone's come up with the real issues. I don't agree with everything you said but I don't dispute your right to say it. And it gives us an agenda to debate. Would anyone like to respond to any of these points?"

I sigh with relief as the subsequent discussion develops these issues further and I find that the majority share my views. I keep quiet, still wondering what the response of Prior and the Chairman will be. The session ends with some comments from the Financial Director. He says that this debate will be part of the input into the final decisions about changes to the system. He thanks our group for stimulating the debate and I can't help feeling pleased with myself. I think that it would have been fun to tell Jean about this if we'd still been together. Moments of real achievement should be shared. Then I remember I can tell Chris – it was she who started me on this path by recommending the book.

We break up and I make my way to the bar. In the doorway I find to my horror that it's almost empty except for Prior and the Chairman. I've got no choice but to join them, and I see the serious look on both their faces. Just then a voice comes over the Tannoy, "Telephone call for Mr Moorley. Mr Moorley of Universal to reception please."

Saved by the bell, I rush to reception and then to the telephone nearby.

"Hello," I say.

"Hello, Phil," a familiar voice comes over the phone, "it's Chris. Sorry to bother you but Harvard have just been on the phone. There's a place come up a term earlier than expected. And I have to make up my mind today."

"Yes, Chris?"

"Well, I want to tell you, to ask you, if it's OK. I do want to take it. I'm really sorry."

"Chris," I say, but without conviction, "it's your career – you must do what you think best. When do you take the place?"

"That's the point, Phil – they want me in five weeks' time."

I hang up the phone and wander back to Prior and the Chairman in the bar. Suddenly I don't give a damn what they think of the presentation. There's only one place I want to be in five weeks' time and that's Boston, Massachusetts.

Chapter 19

I'm sitting at my desk looking at this young woman from Universal who's been put forward as our new Chief Accountant. As soon as I knew Chris wasn't going to change her mind, I decided I must have someone good to head the finance function. My wild ideas about following her to the States soon evaporated, and my commitment to Lawrensons was increased by the warm words of praise from Prior and the Chairman when I returned to the bar. The Chairman even admitted that my ideas had changed his thinking on the subject to some extent – praise indeed!

And now I'm back at Lawrensons with terrible problems on pie sales and the almost impossible task of finding someone to replace Chris. This poor woman's trying to impress but I can't help comparing her. It doesn't help that Chris is sitting next to her, helping me with the interview. She's attractive and confident as ever and, at her side, the other woman seems diffident and mousy. I've a feeling that our new Chief Accountant will have to be a man – a woman will never match up.

"What do you think are the main contributions an accountant can make to company management?" asks Chris.

"Well, the budget," says the prospective applicant, "and the variances."

This seems to be a woman of few words and I've already made up my mind that she's wasting her time. I want to bring the interview quickly to a close, but Chris carries on questioning and I suspect, from her rather sharp manner, that she's also disappointed with the girl's approach.

"Please could you explain a little more," she says. "How do you see the budget helping management? Why do you think the budget is produced?"

"Well, Universal needs budgets by the end of November."

"Yes, but why do you think we want it here?" I ask, trying hard to control my exasperation.

"So we can produce the variances for the monthly reports."

I sit back and decide not to try any more.

Chris perseveres for a while but it's obvious that this girl has no idea of the management accounting role. All she can think of is Universal – no conception of what the operating companies want to help them control the business. This is confirmed by another question which Chris, asks, 'How often do you think we should revise latest estimates of the year's performance?"

"Quarterly," comes the usual one-word answer.

"Why?"

"Universal converted to quarterly updating in 1984".

After Chris has shown the applicant out, she comes back to my office.

"I'd rather have Mike Marshall than that one," I say. "He interviewed far better." Marshall has been encouraged to apply in competition with the applicants put forward by Universal's Group Accountant.

"Just no vision of what management accounting can do," says Chris. "It's because she hasn't come through the Universal graduate training set-up and didn't have the wider business training. She went straight to Universal's Accounts Department after A levels and took the management accounting exams. All they seem to learn about in those exams is variances."

"Yes," I reply, "you must tell me what she was going on about when she mentioned variances. That's something you haven't explained to me."

"I intend to before I go. Now we've got a realistic budget to work on, our variance analysis will be much more meaningful. Though it's all been distorted by the salmonella. Can we fix a time next week? I'll have the January variances and the latest estimates by then."

"I thought that girl said Universal did them quarterly?"

"That's right. It just shows her narrowness. That may be OK for Universal's control but I like to see them monthly to keep on top of things. And the salmonella outbreak alone justifies a revised estimate anyway because we'll never make pie volumes now."

We agree to meet next week and Chris suggests that we involve some of the key managers in the meeting to see what we can do to make up for the lost profit on pies.

It's 5 o'clock and it's Friday evening. The weekend stretches ahead of me. I'm picking up the children tomorrow morning and we're going to London for the day. I'm not looking forward to it because life is still difficult with Mark and Angela. They felt very let down when I messed up their efforts to bring Jean and me together again. On an impulse I say to Chris, "I know you're probably busy packing or something, but how would you like to come to London with my two horrors tomorrow? It's so much easier with someone else there. I thought we could do Madame Tussauds and the zoo."

"I'm not packing yet, Phil. There's still three weeks to go. But I have got to do some shopping – I was planning to go to Oxford Street. Why don't we meet for lunch?"

The weekend suddenly seems more attractive and the following day I find that the reality matches my best hopes. The morning is strained, as it has been each time recently, but the atmosphere changes after we meet Chris. She gets on beautifully with both of them, particularly Angie, and those two go off together to do more shopping while Mark and I go to the Planetarium. I had wondered how the children would react but they don't seem to see Chris as in any way a rival to Jean. Perhaps they see her as closer to their generation than mine. Or maybe they've given up any idea that Jean and I might get together again.

I offer Chris a lift and drop her off before I take the kids home. Since the trauma at the restaurant, I've just delivered them to the house without even seeing Jean and I do the same again today. There'll be a time when I can start to build the bridge again but not today. As I drive home, I think about Angela telling her mother about Oxford Street and all the shopping Chris was doing for the States. I shiver at the thought of Jean's response.

In bed that night, I think again how good Chris was with the kids. I begin to have silly fantasies about Chris, Mark and Angie around a barbecue in the garden of a big house in Boston. Eventually it merges into a confused dream about all of them and Jean too, which only confirms my mixed-up state.

The next week is spent continuing the interviews with potential Chief Accountants and, in between, trying to keep my in-tray moving. I keep getting reports on pie sales but the scare has dealt us a serious blow. Malcolm reckons it will be months before the public has forgotten and everyone sees our pies as safe to eat again.

Our meeting about the budget is on Wednesday morning, just after the last interview. This last applicant is the one I'll probably take – a very earnest young man with a sound view of business, but still falling far short of the standard which Chris has led me to expect. Though it's difficult to know how far my views are coloured by my feelings for her, she certainly is going to be hard to replace. And somehow, half the attraction of the job at Lawrensons will go with her. I despair even more at the thought of being Sales and Marketing Director again.

The meeting consists of Malcolm, Chris, Appleby and me. Martyn Ames is still on his induction programme – spending this week out with a salesman to find out the problems in the field. I'm beginning to think that I misjudged him – he's made a good impression with everyone, buckling down to any task required of him.

Chris starts off the meeting by handing round a paper. It's headed:

January results – variance analysis

		£'000
Budgeted profit		287
Favourable variances		
Material usage	14	
Labour efficiency	8	
Variable factory overheads	3	
Selling expenses	4	
Personnel and training	1	
Extra sales volume on cakes	19	
Higher selling prices on bread	4	53
		340
Unfavourable variances		
Material price	7	
Labour wage rate	4	
Fixed factory overheads	6	
Admin. expenses	2	
Marketing expenses	10	
Other expenses	1	
Lost sales volume on pies	58	
Lost sales volume on bread	4	
Lower selling price on pies	9	
Lower selling price on cakes	2	103
Actual profit		237

For a few minutes we all look at the figures in silence. Then there's a few low whistles and expressions of surprise. We begin to chat about the analysis – everyone has their own comment to make and query to raise. Appleby seems defensive about his fixed overhead spend, saying it's partly the monthly phasing and partly the extra costs caused by the salmonella scare.

I look across at Chris and try to indicate my uncertainty about how to handle this. If we're not careful, it's going to degenerate into an inquest. She nods to me as if to say, "let me say something."

I cut across the chatter and say, "Now hang on a minute, John, Malcolm. This is the first time we've had a variance statement like this so we're all learning together. Chris, would you like to tell us how you think we should use it?"

"Thanks, Phil. Yes, of course. The main reason for analysing variances is to find out where actual performance has differed from budget, how much it has cost us and then, where appropriate, how we can take action to correct the problem."

"But surely, Chris, in many cases you can't do anything about the variances," I say, "particularly this month when we've had the pie problem."

"And material prices," says Appleby. "The price of flour has just shot up without warning. There's nothing we can do about that."

"OK," she replies, "but at least we know what the effect of these factors has been and what we have to recover. We should always be thinking of ways to compensate if we possibly can. For instance, if material prices have gone up, we could think of bringing forward our selling price increases."

"I'm not so sure about that," says Malcolm. "Our customers are expecting an increase on 1 April and I'd prefer not to bring it forward. I'd like to know how these adverse selling price variances are made up, by the way."

"There's a complete analysis for you here, Malcolm. I've got a full set of supporting papers for all of you and I'd like to suggest that you have a detailed look and we can discuss them further at tomorrow's management meeting."

I'm becoming concerned about the negative tones of Malcolm and Appleby so I add, "And let's not make it an inquest where we all make excuses. I want to hear something positive coming out of it to restore the lost profit."

"We can't hope to recover the profit lost on pies, Phil," says Malcolm. "You must accept that."

"Maybe not directly," I say, "but this analysis has shown us other adverse variances which we can work on. And, as

Chris says, we should be looking for all possible ways to help profit."

As I say this, I realize just what the variance analysis is doing. It's telling us about all the causes of differences from budget and giving them a price tag. But for Chris's analysis, we would have blamed all the lost profit on pies and not looked at the other things which have varied from budget.

Chris is leaning forward as if she wants to say something else. I nod to her.

"I've projected the year's results assuming that we don't take specific action to compensate. Malcolm gave me likely pie sales volumes and I've calculated cost levels where the January figures indicate significant variances for the year as a whole. It shows us exactly what we have to recover during the year if we are to make our budgeted profit. I think the pie crisis does justify a re-think of our budget assumptions. I'm sorry I won't be here to help you implement it."

I don't need reminding about that. I know only too well that she'll be gone in just over two weeks' time. The paper she passes around is headed:

Revised estimate

	Year's budget	Latest estimate
Sales	117,901	117,387
Variable costs	81,406	81,065
Contribution	36,495	36,322
Fixed production	8,429	8,429
Profit before indirects	28,066	27,893
Administration	7,200	7,200
Research & devl.	1,238	1,238
Sales	7,936	7,924
Marketing	3,672	3,732
Personnel	811	811
Others	3,251	3,251
Total indirects	24,108	24,156
Profit before tax	3,958	3,737

I recall the budget figures from my final budget meeting with Prior. Now we look like losing nearly a quarter of a million profit and the year's hardly started. Sales are down – I anticipated that. Half a million is about what we expect to lose on pies before we get back to our budgeted levels. But I can't understand the differences on sales and marketing costs. I ask Chris about this.

"The sales expense saving is the likely delay in recruitment. We assumed the new salesmen in London from the beginning of the year and there's no way they'll be in place before April. Isn't that right, Malcolm?"

Malcolm nods and adds, "The marketing cost increase is from me, Phil. I suggested that Chris put in £50,000 for extra advertising to boost pie volume. I don't think we'll make the levels in the revised estimate without going on TV. I'm not sure about the other £10,000, Chris. The total difference is £60,000."

"It's what you've already spent over budget in January. Remember the variance analysis I've given you shows £10,000 overspent. That was to promote pies in the week after the crisis. In-store merchandizing mainly, wasn't it?"

I'm beginning to see the further power of variance analysis as it draws our attention to the financial effect of each decision we make. I remember agreeing to in-store merchandizing but I'd no idea it cost as much as that. I also see how important it was for Chris to calculate the revised estimate. It shows what we have to do if we are to get back to the budgeted profit. If I'm to be MD of Lawrensons, I want to make sure I deliver budgeted profit in my first year. I say to the others, "I want to know how we're going to recover that £221,000 shortfall from the year's budget. This estimate assumes we do nothing different – I'm not going to sit back and accept the loss of profit. And I want genuine realistic plans, not pie in the sky."

I hadn't noticed the pun, but laughing releases the tension. I think the three of them are quite surprised at the intensity with which I asked for their profit improvement ideas, but maybe they underestimate my commitment. Now that Chris is going and my family seem destined to keep distant from me, I have to make a go of this.

As they get up to leave, I ask Chris to stay. Malcolm and Appleby give each other a knowing look – it's become quite a familiar pattern for Chris to stay behind with me after meetings. I only wish it had been what the gossip-mongers suspect. Instead it is, as usual, to ask her to explain a financial concept.

"Chris, that variance analysis was very useful but I'd like to know a bit more about how you get the figures. Talking about material price and usage variances is all very well, but how are they calculated?"

"It can be very complex, but I'll try to explain the basic principles. As long as you understand the general idea, that's the main thing."

She walks over to my whiteboard and takes up her familiar stance, felt pen in hand.

"The objective is to split the different causes of variances from budget and put a price tag on each one. Thus, for example, John Appleby would know which of his managers to take problems up with. The Buying Manager for the price variance, the Materials Controller for usage."

"Or even find out that part of the variance is uncontrollable, like price inflation," I add.

"Yes. In which case he can concentrate on the controllable part and also know what has to be recovered if budgeted profit is to be achieved," she replies. "Let's take some simple figures and I'll use materials as an example."

She writes up:

Budgeted materials = 130 tons at £100 per ton = £13,000
Actual materials   = 140 tons at £105 per ton = £14,700
Total material cost variance   (1,700)

"OK," she says, "what are the two causes of the variance?"

"Price and consumption."

"Good. We usually call it price and usage."

She writes up:

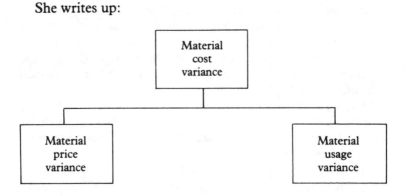

"Now, Phil, we have to split the 1,700 between price and usage. Can you tell me the price variance?"

"£5."

"That's per ton. What about the total effect?"

"£5 times 130 tons, I suppose."

"No, it's not actually, Phil. You could argue that it should be. But the formula normally used is price difference times *actual* usage. Each ton of material used has cost you £5 over budget and you've used 140 so the total effect of price being over budget is £5 times £140."

She writes up:

MATERIAL PRICE VARIANCE

Price difference × Actual usage
£5 × £140 = (700) Adverse

"That's the price variance. So the usage variance must be £1,000 because the total adverse cost variance is £1,700 and we've identified £700 for price. But can you see how the £1,000 is calculated?"

I'm beginning to grasp the idea. We've taken out the price difference, so it must be standard price multiplied by the usage difference. We've used 10 tons extra and each one cost £100 per ton.

"Well done," Chris says and writes up:

MATERIAL USAGE VARIANCE

Usage difference × Standard price
   10   ×   £100   = (£1,000) adverse

Then she enters in the boxes:

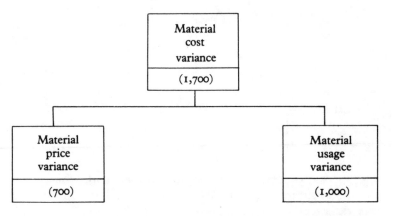

"So Appleby can know how hard to kick the backside of his Buying Manager and his Material Controller," I say.

"You could say that. Or at least where to target his effort. In some cases the total variance might be favourable but the analysis could reveal an adverse usage variance which is hidden by a saving on price. Then variance analysis is essential to help the manager tackle problems which he might otherwise miss."

"Is that all I need to know?" I ask.

"In a way, yes. The overhead variances are fairly simple, though with variable overhead, as with all variable costs, I have to take out the effect of volume before making the cost comparison. It might be worth showing you the labour variances – they're the other important ones in addition to materials".

She writes:

> Budgeted labour = 40 hours at £5 = £200
> Actual labour = 38 hours at £6 = £228
> Total labour cost variance   (£28)

Then she adds:

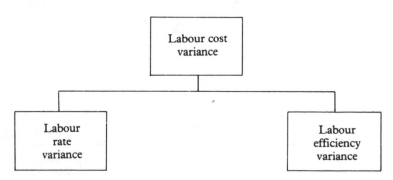

"Now," says Chris, "you should be able to do these. We use the same principle as with materials. What's the labour rate variance?"

By now it's becoming much easier to understand. I say, "Rate variance is excess rate of £1 per hour for the actual hours of 38–£38. And efficiency variance is the difference of two hours at the standard rate of £5 – that's £10. £38 plus £10 is £48."

"No, Phil. The £10 is favourable. You work two hours less than standard and save £10. It reconciles to the total cost variance of £28 because the £10 saving cancels out some of the adverse effect of the rate."

She writes in the boxes:

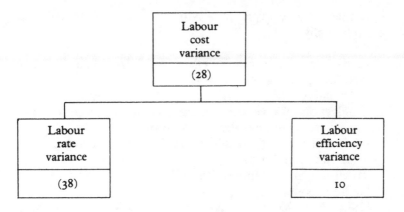

"If you can follow these principles, it's about as much as you need to know. I, my staff and the computer do the rest."

"But what about the sales variances? The loss of pie volume? How did you calculate that one?"

"That gets very complex and I'm still trying to perfect it. In fact there are three sales variances – volume, price and mix – but I haven't yet programmed the computer to calculate mix. My successor will have to do that. At present I extract any variance due to sales price being different from budget, then I calculate the balance as contribution lost because of volume."

"Contribution?"

"Yes, that's what you lose when volume is down. Sales less variable costs. You lose sales but you save the variable costs, so the effect on profit is the difference."

"Because fixed costs stay the same?"

"Right."

"Phew," I say, "my brain's hurting but I think I know enough to use the data. Thanks for your help."

"That's OK. I just hope my successor continues to do the analysis for you."

This reminds me of something which is always there at the back of my mind but which I try not to think about. In about two weeks she'll be gone.

Just then the phone rings. Sylvia's gone to lunch and the line's been put through.

A man's voice says, "Mr Moorley, can I speak to you confidentially?"

"Yes."

Chris hovers, not sure whether to go. I ought to tell her to but, for some reason, I don't.

"My name is Michael Lloyds of Morgan Bennett, Executive Selection. We've been given your name in connection with a position which we're trying to fill."

Chris still stands there and I still don't ask her to go.

"Tell me more," I say.

"Well, it's in the United States."

"Whereabouts?"

"Near New York, Mr Moorley. It's a food company. I can't mention names but a new Chief Executive has been recently appointed and wants a Vice President, Sales and Marketing. I believe he's met you."

Of course, Richard Watts. He said he was going to leave Universal.

"Are you there, Mr Moorley?" I say yes and he continues.

"It's 100,000 dollars a year, Mr Moorley, and I'm assured the job is well within your range and experience."

Yes, well within. Sales and marketing. What I can do well and what I can do easily, without stretching myself too much. But without the involvement and excitement which comes with being in the MD's chair. And Richard is younger than me so I'll be unlikely to make the top job if I go to the States.

Then I see Chris looking quizzically at me, half smiling, so young and alive. What a fool I've been.

I suddenly know with absolute certainty what I have to do. I'll go to the States, leave Lawrensons and my recent traumatic past behind me. And I know who I want to go with.

Chapter 20

I'm standing at the check-in desk for the 14.00 Pan-Am flight to Boston. Chris is standing next to me, her cases on the trolley at the side. The checking-in time of the people in front of us seems interminable, but there's still an hour and a half before take-off.

I look at her. "You know something," I say, "I'm going to miss you."

"It's mutual," she replies with a trace of embarrassment, "but we'll see each other again when you come over. How long do you reckon that will be?"

"About six weeks. The new MD starts on Monday and the handover will take quite a while."

"It really is kind of you to see me off, Phil," she says. "You needn't have bothered."

"No problem. The children wanted to come and we couldn't let you go off on your own."

"Yes. That would have been grim. My parents live so far away, otherwise they'd have made it."

There's an awkward silence for a few seconds while I try to think of something to say.

"Where are the children?" asks Chris. "I'd like to say goodbye to them before I go."

"They'll be back in a moment. They've just gone to get a magazine each."

"It will be great to see them in the States," Chris says, "It's funny how things have worked out."

Just then Angela and Mark return, looking happy and excited. They've only been to an airport a few times before and they're enjoying every minute.

"Well, did you find any?" I ask.

"Yes, Dad," says Angela, "and I've got *Vogue* for Mum with the change. I hope that's all right."

"Of course," I reply. *Vogue* always was Jean's favourite magazine, though she'd rarely want to lash out on the clothes she read about.

I look at my watch. I've promised to have the children home for lunch. I say to them, "You say goodbye to Chris now and I'll join you in the car in five minutes."

They say goodbye with genuine affection and are very excited when Chris says that she'll invite them to Harvard.

After they've gone I turn to her and say, "Chris. There's something I'd like to say before you go. It'll probably embarrass both of us but I'm going to say it anyway."

"Fire away," she says, "and I'll try not to be embarrassed." She smiles encouragingly.

"Well, it's just that I'd like to thank you for all the help you've given me. You were around when I needed a friend to talk to and you did wonders for my confidence just when I needed it most. And, in ways which it's difficult to explain, you made me think very deeply about my life."

"Thanks, Phil. I didn't do very much at all but it's sweet of you to say so. And I'm truly delighted about you and Jean getting together again. I hope you'll be very happy with your new life in the States. And that you'll let me come and see you."

I know I ought to leave it at that but something inside me makes me want to tell her everything.

"There's something else you ought to know, Chris. Before I decided to leave Lawrensons and go back to Jean, I did – well – feel something for you or thought I did. I was very near telling you several times but you made it clear you only wanted friendship."

She turns away, looking embarrassed, and I think that maybe I should have kept my big mouth shut.

"I'm glad you didn't tell me how you felt, Phil. Because I'm sure I wouldn't have resisted very hard."

"You mean that you felt the same?"

"I thought you were fantastic from the first time I saw you. You don't think I give up my evenings for finance lessons for just anyone, do you? But after a while I decided I had to keep you at arm's length because I knew what would happen. And I'd been hurt very badly just before I came to Lawrensons."

All reason tells me that I ought to leave it there but I find myself asking. "How?"

"I was in love with someone else. He was older than me too."

"And?"

"I found out he was married. After I told him I was pregnant."

"Excuse me," a voice says. "Would you like to check in now?"

We haven't noticed that the person in front has finished and it's Chris's turn to check in.

As she hands over her ticket and answers a series of questions, I think over what she's just told me and what it must have cost her to say. Perhaps she wanted to tell me everything before she went, the way I did. I think about her as a poor, vulnerable girl who was badly hurt and find it hard to reconcile with her confident, organized image at Lawrensons. I wonder how well you ever know anybody.

But I also think about myself. How I'd been lacking the confidence to develop a relationship with her which I could have had all the time if I'd tried. But things have worked out for the best. A job I can easily cope with, a new environment and my family together. That must be right, mustn't it?

After she's checked in her bags, we turn to each other to say goodbye. I sense that she doesn't want to talk any more and I resist asking the other questions which stir in my mind. We kiss on the cheek like the friends we are and agree that I'll ring her when we're settled in New York. I watch her walk briskly to the departure gate, suddenly a lonely figure among the crowds of people rushing all ways across the terminal.

Next Monday I'm in my office talking to Brian Ridgway, the new MD of Lawrensons. This was confirmed two weeks after I gave in my resignation and after Prior had received confirmation from Jim's doctor that he wasn't going to be fit to return to work in the foreseeable future and that early retirement was the only option.

Brian seems a reasonable sort of chap. He's been MD of Universal's margarine operation for some years and is now in his mid-fifties. He's obviously the caretaker, for Martyn Ames to take over in a few years' time.

He tells me about his new house and I remark how quickly he's organized things.

"Yes," he says, "we only started looking in early December."

More than a month before I handed in my resignation!

Later that afternoon, Prior's in my office. I decide to confront him.

"Paul," I say, "Brian tells me that he knew about becoming MD early in December. Is that right? He was coming here even if I hadn't resigned?"

Prior looks at me and nods.

"Afraid so, Phil," he replies. "You never had a real chance. I tried to hint this to you several times. We hardly ever promote people to MD if they've come through the ranks in one company. It's company policy – you must have heard the Personnel Director talking about it on your course. But you'd have got an MD's job in Universal within a few years. Your performance as acting MD saw to that. You made quite an impression on the Chairman."

Six weeks later, I'm sitting in a Boeing 747. Jean is in the window seat and we're holding hands like teenagers. It's been like that since we came together again. The kids are in the seats in front.

"You know, Phil," she says, "I'm not sure I should have made that condition about you always putting us first in future."

"You were right, love. Otherwise we'll never have a chance to make a go of things."

"But you love your work. You were obviously enjoying every minute when you were MD at Lawrensons. Will you be happy with less?"

"I told you, Jean. I wouldn't have become MD anyway. And the new job will be different. It's sales and marketing, which I know best, and there's a new challenge too. Believe it o. not, Richard wants the Chief Accountant to report to me."

Jean's expression seems to combine hope with doubt. "hope it's enough for you."

"I'm sure it will be, love," I reply, "and I've got m family back. That's the bottom line. It makes up for ever thing."

As the plane taxies down the runway, I wonder if, de down, I really believe it.

Index

Management Training Partnership

Since its formation in 1987, MTP has grown rapidly to become the largest UK provider of tailored management training outside the business schools. Indeed for many of its major company clients it has become a preferable high value alternative to traditional academic programmes.

The main areas of focus are:

- finance and management accounting
- marketing
- human resource management
- business management programmes which integrate these core topics within tailored, innovative course designs.

The client list is evidence of the success which MTP has achieved and includes:

- Unilever
- Marks & Spencer
- British Airways
- Smith Kline Beecham

The innovative and practical nature of this book – written by one of MTP's founding partners – is a good example of our ability to provide user-friendly and effective learning for your managers.

For further information, please contact:

Alan Warner
Management Training Partnership plc
3 Prebendal Court
Oxford Road
Aylesbury
Bucks   HP19 3EY
England

Telephone: 0296 23474   Facsimile: 0296 393879

Becoming the Best

How to Gain Company-wide
Commitment to Total Quality

Barry Popplewell and Alan Wildsmith

How could it happen in a buoyant market? New products, lots of orders, and yet no profit – a big fat ZERO. The opportunity had been there – and he'd blown it. As the story unfolds Neil begins to understand the problem.

Quality is the key – not just product quality but total quality. "If everybody was the best at what they do," he thought " then this would be one hell of a company." So that's what he sets out to do – become the best. How he conceives his idea, translates it into practice, cajoles and carries his employees with him, is all in this fascinating book.

Contents
"The day had started bad. It couldn't get any worse."; "Facts...the bright stepping stones of logic."; "No problem's too big. What it needs is a big solution, and the will to do it."; "What it means is, you're not in control."; "One common aim for everybody."; "The organization was rife with rumour."; "He didn't want a navigation officer, he wanted a bomb-disposal squad."; "Improve the whole organization, everybody, everywhere. Impossible?"; "This whole organization is going to be turned upside down."; "Everybody is a supplier and a customer."; "Enthusiasm, a sense of purpose, you don't generate those by pushing a piece of paper under somebody's nose."; "Basic questions like 'Do you know who your customers are?'"; "No more red-label orders, no panics. What a sweet life."; "Best in the world applies to people, not things."; "Hold on to your vision. Stay with it". Epilogue.

1988   156 pages   0 566 02798 4 Hardback   0 566 02877 8 Paperback

Gower

Beyond the Bottom Line

Advanced Financial Management in Business

Alan Warner

A Gower Novel

In this fascinating sequel to The Bottom Line Phil Moorley finds himself president of a large US food manufacturer, and facing a takeover bid from Universal, his previous employer. He finds that the financial knowledge acquired in The Bottom Line is not enough to cope with this new challenge. As before, he turns for help to blonde, beautiful management consultant Christine Goodhart. The takeover bid is resolved and, in the course of it, the reader learns about: • evaluating an acquisition • price/earnings ratio and market capitalization • treatment of goodwill • asset valuations, including brands • dividend yield and dividend cover • the factors affecting share price.

Moorley offers Christine the job as his VP Finance, with consequences which do more for his company than for his marriage. The second half of the book describes how Phil and Christine work together to develop improved management accounting information systems to support their strategic decision-making. The subjects covered include: • principles of financial measurement • replacement cost accounting • limiting factor analysis • price/volume sensitivities • ratios for competitor analysis • Pareto analysis of product/customer profiles • strategic profitability evaluations • post audit of investment appraisals • direct product profitability techniques.

Readers will find that they are able to consolidate the knowledge gained from The Bottom Line and be introduced to some advanced but practical concepts of finance rarely dealt with in conventional textbooks.

1992   231 pages   0 566 0265 3 Hardback   0 566 07479 6 Paperback

Gower

The Focused Business Plan

Vandenburghs Chartered Accountants

The Focused Business Plan is a highly practical and readable guide to evaluating a business from the vantage points of sales/costs/cash and assimilating that information into a clearly defined business strategy. It guides you through the initial stages of why the business plan is essential and who should prepare it, to establishing basic information, concentrating on specific areas of the plan and eventually, to who the users are and how the plan should best be presented to them. Model plans are used to illustrate the various stages.

Contents

Introduction • First steps to planning • The steps of an effective plan • Who should prepare the plan • Under-standing why the business plan document works •Contents of the business plan document • Describing the company • The target • Funding requirements •Dealing with risk •Devising the plan • The sales and margins plan • The overheads plan • The funding plan • The right type of funding • Focusing the plan • Risk • Handling risk • What the users think • Investors • Bank managers • Lawyers • Accountants • Examples • The business plans • The City University Business School plan • DuBoulay Construction Limited plan.

1992   186 pages   0 566 07286 6

Gower

The Goal

Beating the Competition
Second Edition

Eliyahu M Goldratt and Jeff Cox

Written in a fast-paced thriller style, *The Goal* is the gripping novel which is transforming management thinking throughout the Western world.

Alex Rogo is a harried plant manager working ever more desperately to try to improve performance. His factory is rapidly heading for disaster. So is his marriage. He has ninety days to save his plant - or it will be closed by corporate HQ, with hundreds of job losses. It takes a chance meeting with a colleague from student days - Jonah - to help him break out of conventional ways of thinking to see what needs to be done.

The story of Alex's fight to save his plant is more than compulsive reading. It contains a serious message for all managers in industry and explains the ideas which underlie the Theory of Constraints (TOC) developed by Eli Goldratt - the author described by Fortune as 'a guru to industry' and by Businessweek as a 'genius'.

As a result of the phenomenal and continuing success of *The Goal*, there has been growing demand for a follow-up. Eliyahu Goldratt has now written ten further chapters which continues the story of Alex Rogo as he makes the transition from Plant Manager to Divisional Manager. Having achieved the turnround of his plant, Alex now attempts to apply all that Jonah has taught him, not to crisis management, but to ongoing improvement.

These new chapters reinforce the thinking process utilised in the first edition of *The Goal* and apply them to a wider management context with the aim of stimulating readers into using the technique in their own environment.

1993   352 pages   0 566 07417 6 Hardback   0 566 07418 4 Paperback

Gower

Managing Mergers and Acquisitions
A Practical Guide to Managing Domestic and Cross Border Company Integration

Ann McDonagh Bengtsson

Acquiring may be more fun than managing, but in the 1990s businesses cannot afford to buy companies then sub-optimize their investment through shoddy management. And it is never too late to repair past mistakes. Nobody knows better than practitioners what makes mergers and acquisitions work or how it feels to face furious shareholders at the AGM when they do not. This is the real world of M&As – success, failure and above all, accountability. Top European managers uninhibitedly contribute ideas, reflections and experience. Their practical views are synthesised by a European management consultant into a highly readable aid to successful management of M&As. Practical guidelines and illustrative comments applicable to all acquisitions are complemented by a separate section on cross border deals. International target selection, negotiation, cultural awareness and the realities of doing business in risky places are among the topics covered. Case studies in the words of four presidents, one vice-president and three senior directors from six contrasting business heritages add insight into M&A policy and practice in some of Europe's most interesting companies.

Contents

Acknowledgements; Introduction; Part One: Preparation, Principles and Practice; Section A – Preparing for success; Section B – Making the merger work; Section C – Managing people – a key factor; Section D – Consolidation; Part Two: Cross Border Acquisitions; Part Three: Case Studies; Appendices.

1992   192 pages   0 566 07304 8

Gower